Memoirs of a
Free Pilgrim

— P I L G R I M —

 FriesenPress

Suite 300 - 990 Fort St
Victoria, BC, V8V 3K2
Canada

www.friesenpress.com

ISBN
978-1-03-911375-6 (Hardcover)
978-1-03-911374-9 (Paperback)
978-1-03-911376-3 (eBook)

1. Biography & Autobiography, Personal Memoirs

Distributed to the trade by The Ingram Book Company

Contents

For May, my loving wife and constant companion with whom I share the joy -

For my understanding children Selena and Nigel from their imperfect father -

For my dear relatives who live their lives fullest in sorrow, happiness, and joy -

A family relationship is a gift. It is the "gladness of our being."

Memoirs
of
a Free Pilgrim

The story begins

Westwood Plateau Golf Course Coquitlam B.C and beyond.

Autumn was upon us once again. The leaves of the maple trees in Coquitlam had already turned to hue of red and gold, many fallen and scattered on the ground below. On this unusual sunny day in British Columbia, golden rays pierced through the leaves of the Ponderosa pines growing majestically on the Westwood Plateau Golf Course. I was sitting at the breakfast nook in my house on Caulfield Ridge, with a large warm croissant in my left hand and a mug of hot home-brewed dark and bold coffee on the right. Butter, marmalade, and brown sugar on the round glass-top breakfast table. This was an unusual morning for me. At this time of the day, I would normally be having toasts and drinking a mug of strong Lipton Yellow Label Tea or Van Cheong's Fine Tea (the Hong-Kong Style Tea), brewed exactly right, from loose tea leaves, not tea bags. Instead of fresh milk and white sugar, I used Eagle Brand (original) sweetened condensed milk. A flavour and taste which I had long acquired while living in Malaysia.

But sometimes, I would use English Breakfast tea, customarily pour milk in the cup first, then the tea, and then add two little cubes of white sugar. Today, tea is not important. I looked down the valley and slowly moved my eyes to try to see beyond the Fraser River. But the fog had not lifted. I could barely see Mount Baker that lay beyond. It somehow brought back memories of Mount Kinabalu, the tallest mountain in South East Asia, located in Sabah. Sabah is one of the Malaysian states and, together with Sarawak, form the region commonly called East Malaysia. It is located on the northern portion of Borneo - the third largest island in the world. It borders with Brunei and Sarawak to the southwest and Indonesia's Kalimantan region to the south.

A picture was being formed. There I was, rising early and sitting at the terrace overlooking the Likas Sports Complex, listening to the birds singing nearby and surrounded by clay pots of colourful bougainvillea at 76 Signal Hill, Kota Kinabalu (KK as it is fondly called) Sabah. This was my favourite time of the day in KK. It was cool, until the hot tropical sun rose high above Mount Kinabalu's peaks, visible beyond Likas Bay. Here I was, relaxing in Coquitlam and thinking. We travel the world, traversing, globetrotting, and peregrinating, from one place to another, enjoying the glittery life in big cities and metropoles while the unique and simple life we once lived is all but almost forgotten. This seemed a good day for me to reflect, take a step back, and frame pictures with memories of days gone by, from the mundane to the more interesting, the pleasant, and the not so.

I have always preferred to listen to others telling stories than to write one myself. This story is not intended to be an autobiography. So, I apologize if readers miss some events during my tenure in the public service or the time in my private life. To me, an autobiographer should have total openness and humility, two human characters of which I am in short supply. We are human. Memories do fail us or play tricks on us. What we write may not precisely be what had happened. Besides, one should avoid giving weight to an autobiography when the author writes about others, particularly about those they might have had issues with or worst still, if at the time of writing they still harbour animosity towards. I hope that I do not fall into the trap of disloyalty, as some writers did after they retired from public service, some to the point of dishonourably breaking confidentiality to sell their books. To me, a complete and true autobiography is one which the writer would like Almighty God to be the only reader. I hope what I write here may have some meaning, but I am not sure it has. Even if it has, I think readers of this book may find the meaning different or worse than I had intended.

Background

The year was 1945, and the Second World War (WWII) had just ended. It was more than 70 years ago. If you did not live through it, you would never understand. Let me back up a little. I was barely three years old. "Ah, Chung, ngee oi mao (do you want it)?" my paternal grandma asked. We spoke in Hakka - a Chinese dialect. "ng moi (no)," I answered, thinking it was another piece of boiled tapioca root. "jook whoa (it's rice porridge)," she said. "ngai oi, ngai oi (I want, I want!)". I ran to her and took the half bowl of rice porridge from her stretched hand. I was too young to have a memory of this incident. This incident had been related to me many times over by my grandmother when I was older. I was born into a large family of fifteen siblings. The fifth child. The second son. It was not the best time to be born. It was a challenging time. It was a dangerous time.

On the 2nd of January 1942, the Japanese forces invaded British North Borneo (Sabah) without resistance by way of Mempakut and Weston on the west coast. They reached Sandakan, the Capitol of the State on the 9th day of January 1942. They then suspended the British North Borneo Company's administration. The Japanese Military Government occupied and assumed the administration of the territory. The occupation lasted for almost four years until the Battle of North Borneo (part of the broader Borneo Campaign of the Pacific

War). This Battle was fought fiercely between the Allied and the Japanese forces from 10 June to 15 August 1945.

On the 10th day of June 1945, the Allied Forces landed in Labuan in the Japanese strong opposition's face. After extensive military operations, the Allied Forces re-occupied part and later the whole of North Borneo. Martial law was proclaimed by the British Military Administration, canceling all legislative enactments of whatever kind issued by the Japanese Military Government. For administrative convenience, North Borneo was administered as part of "British Borneo," which included the State of North Borneo's territories, the Settlement of Labuan, and the State of Sarawak. Naturally, I had no recollection of the war. I was too young. I was told that we survived the war sustaining on tapioca roots, sweet potatoes, and leaves. When I was older, I noticed the bullet marks of machine guns left on our wooden house walls. I saw what was left of a burrow under our house. There was a dugout for shelter at the hill close to our home.

The wooden house

Our wooden house

Our family lost the house they used to live in before WWII in downtown Sandakan. I never knew whether it was ever commissioned for use by the Japanese Army. It was no longer there after the war. It appeared to have been burned, either by bombardments during the war or burned down deliberately. During my childhood, I remember seeing the ruin or the remnant of the house with its clustered pillars standing by Leila Road. This location was the spot where our downtown house used to be and where eventually the Dato House (a block of flats) was constructed thereon.

When the war started, my family relocated to and took shelter in the interior. We grew up in this 2-story wooden house with atap roof (later upgraded to zinc sheets roofing), constructed within a rubber plantation of about 85 acres. The house was rectangular in shape, with two bedrooms on the upper level and another rectangular section added on a few years later as my family grew. There was a ladder alongside the wall of one of the bedrooms my grandmother used when she was living. The ladder was for climbing up to a loft, which acted as an extra sleeping space. There were also two large bedrooms on the lower level: one for the boys and the girls. There was a horizontal fold-down door at the staircase's top—the stairs which led up to the living room directly from the ground below. The builder later moved the stairs when the house was enlarged.

A Durian tree in Sabah

My father or the builders did not think of outside appearance or having a lovely porch, not even about the windows' positions. They had planned the rooms as what was required. All the rooms had the usual old-fashioned beams across. I loved to see these beams across the ceiling. A beam or two or even more above the head and across is a pleasing sight to me even today. We slept on bunk beds, sometimes with falling mosquito nets. When I was little, I could hear creaking sounds coming from the wooden stairs or the floorboards. There was whistling at the windows or mysterious noises coming from under the roof. No dwelling house has the mystic and rustic beauty more than that of our old wooden house. I might make endless comparisons even though some people say comparisons are odious! I suppose we should be content that we have progressed.

However, as a lover of so much that is homelike and simple, I cannot but feel that progress is not always all gain. At least to my mind, it is a fact that how much we have gained in wealth, we have lost much that is romantic and beautiful. Our old simple kampong life was compensated by free space. We had a largely undeveloped area behind the warehouse where I learned and practised javelin throw. I was the javelin record holder (at 174 ft 3 inches) in the Sandakan Amateur Athletic Association (AAA) sports until someone broke it in the late 1950s. Behind our house was a basketball court (albeit on hard clay ground and not cement). We had a sawdust pit at which we practised long jump, hop, step, jump (triple jump), high jump, and pole vault. We had the thrill of picking up the durian fruits which had fallen from the tree the night before. We had the joy of looking at the softened sunlight through the rambutan trees' countless green leaves, the beauty of bamboo plants in front of our house, and the grass fluttering and bending over by the kampong breeze. We smelled the scent of the calamansi...

We lived a simple but happy life, building our seesaw with a tree trunk and a wooden plank. We played games of hide and seek, not only inside the house but sometimes also outside. It was fun, but it could be scary at times. One night when my parents had gone out to Cathay cinema to watch a movie, we went outside to play hide and seek. It was a quiet moonlit night. I was hiding behind a banana tree and waiting... hiding and waiting like children do in hide and seek. I felt sleepy. I nearly dropped off to sleep when I thought I heard some noise coming from the depth of the woods behind me. I turned my head and bent myself nearer to the ground. I thought I heard some soft beating sound or a hissing sound I could not tell. Then the noise became louder. I was so scared. I got goosebumps. I turned and fled and ran as quickly as my 10-year-old legs could carry me back to the safety of our house. Several years ago, we went back to the area, and I noticed that our old wooden house had disappeared entirely...but the memory of it lives on...

Life in Sibuga

I was already asleep. The sound of commotions awoke me. I heard someone shouting, "Bring me the spear!" I jumped down from my upper bunk and ran outside. It was dark, and I could barely see. The chickens in the chicken shed had been making considerable noise of distress. I followed to see what was going on. There, inside the shed, with the help of a torchlight, we saw a well-fed python, at least 12 feet in length, half encircled itself. One of my older cousins speared its head and pinned it to the ground, and it fought fiercely, circling the spear. The chickens were desperate. They flapped their wing - loose feathers flying in the air. The python struggled and eventually became limp. It died. My cousin carried it to the long wooden table in the kitchen. "Get me a knife," someone said. I saw the snake being slit opened, and there was a whole chicken in its stomach. We ended up eating part of the snake cooked and fried with ginger, onions, and soya sauce. The other part was cooked in rice porridge with ginger. It tasted like chicken!

Besides rubbers trees, we started to plant corn, mango, lemons, calamansi, sugarcane, coconut, durians, and tarap - a plant native to Borneo, Palawan. Mindanao in the Philippines. The tarap tree bears fruit like jackfruit or breadfruit. Some old indigenous or rubber trees lived their years, lost their leaves, died, and eventually fell to the ground even without the help of tropical storms. Before these trees dry up, we would saw their branches and them carry back to a Smoke House. The Smoke House, constructed on a small hill behind our home, was to smoke the corrugated rubber sheets we had made from the rubber trees' latex. The rubber sheets' natural rubber material was harvested from the rubber trees we had planted in our area by process of extraction- by manually tapping the trunk of the rubber trees. This process needs further explanation. We will talk about that another time. The trunks of these fallen trees would take a while to dry, but they would eventually all dry up under the burning heat of the tropical sun. Some trunks of the indigenous tree were too heavy to be moved by hands. We had to burn them so that the land could be cleared. We were also hoping to kill two birds with one stone. We cleared the ground for planting and used the ash as fertilizer.

It was in the late 1940 and early 1950. This time was during one of the planting seasons after the war. Someone shouted from across the field: "Ah Chung, can you light the fire and burn that trunk?" Usually, I would answer "OK" without hesitation. Burning the tree trunk was the best part of my job. I enjoyed lighting fire. We did not do shifting cultivation, but we did have to clear the land to plant coconuts, corns, and tapioca. But this was my favorite tree trunk lying in the field. It was enormous. This trunk's diameter must have been at least four feet, and it was hollow. I could easily crawl my way through it. That was fun. This time I said the "OK" with a pang in my heart. My favourite trunk would now be turned into ash. I gathered some dried leaves, piled them up inside the hollow, and poured some kerosene on them. I struck the match and threw it on the leaves. The leaves started to glow, and the glow then turned into flames. Slowly but surely, the inside of the trunk began to burn. The flames sparked, dancing up and down the inside of the trunk, and crackling as I added more dried leaves. I spent the rest of the morning nearby, watching the fire burned through the trunk, and eventually, the outer part of the trunk collapsed.

It was already lunchtime. The cinders were red hot, and we could roast our corns on them. We left the cinders overnight, and we knew not of fire hazards. If they were entirely extinguished by nature, they would be rekindled again by us the next day, and this process was repeated until the trunk had been completely turned to ashes. But today, I was in no hurry to go home. I stayed and watched what was left of my favourite trunk. The land had been cleared and was now an open field ready for planting. The setting sun turned to golden red and began to disappear into the distant horizon. We were near the equator. It did not linger. Suddenly it was out of sight.

After I moved to London, I missed many of the beauties in Kampong's life in Sibuga. When I walked down Piccadilly or Oxford Street, I could not see (let alone observe) the beautiful sunsets. When the British drizzles turned into showers, I would hastily seek shelter in the nearby shops. In Sibuga, when there was a burst of the tropical storm (raining cats and dogs, as they say), I would rush out into the pouring rain, unafraid of the flashes of lightning. The tropical pouring rain would stop suddenly. Then a rainbow would be seen, a lovely sight indeed. The leaves of the rubber trees around us would all hold sparkling drops of crystals, opals, emeralds, topaz, and pearls, or at least I imagined them to be.

Simple joy

Our house was situated about thirty yards from a river that semi-circled around it. The water source was many hundred yards upstream. The water came from natural springs at the head, which flowed down the granite rocks' hard sloping surface and collected into a pond below. There, deep inside the rainforest of Sibuga, was this natural reservoir. As a teenager, I ventured out to these rocky slopes and lay there to feel the pleasant cool water flowing down my back. These slopes could also be slippery. The thrill was also to slide down these slopes into the pond below. However, nothing beats the excitement of swimming in a fast-flowing swollen river after the tropical downpour. Someone shouted, "Grab the coconut." This was the high light for us after the monsoons swelled up the river in front of our house. We would grab a dry coconut upstream and float with it all the way down to the wooden bridge in front of our home. We then disappeared under the bridge momentarily and reappeared on the other side with a victorious up-stretched hand. In later years, the government acquired the area upstream by compulsory acquisition in the public interest and turned it into an official Water Catchment Area.

I still remember that we had to walk along the riverbanks to the water source and followed it upstream. Intermittently we had to walk through some undergrowth. One day as I was walking with my brother George to the water source, I felt a sharp pain in my right ankle and saw a snake slithered through the undergrowth. I instinctively knew the snake had bitten me. "A snake bit me!" I yelled. Brother George was a boy scout. I think he had also learned some survival skills. He always carried with him what he called his "Tarzan" knife on this kind of outings. "You need to get the blood out," my brother said to me. He took his knife and slit across at the bite marks and squeezed out more blood. With my brother's help, I limped my way home. The pain was excruciating. I put iodine on my wound and bandaged my whole ankle. We were not totally holed up in a cocoon that some safe childhood might bestow. Either the snake was not a poisonous one, or my brother's first aid worked. I survived.

Life was not easy

A flushed toilet did not exist for us. We had an outdoor latrine, a little shed with a hanging canvas as the door. Simplicity at its core - two wooden footrests, one on each side above the pit, manually dug. There was always a bucket of sawdust or sand by the side of the shed. Civilized people always try to cover their excrements. An old newspaper of some kind would be handy, although I lack memory of this part of the exercise. New pits would be dug, and the shed moved to the new locations from time to time. At night we used kerosene lamps at home. When I was about ten years old, I read a story and saw Che Yin's picture in a children's book. He was an intelligent kid who grew up in a poor family in ancient China. He loved to read but very often, the family could not afford oil to light a lamp for him to study at night. One night, when he saw fireflies outside his house, he came up with the idea of trapping them in a cloth bag and hanging it up as a lamp. Legend had it that he spent nights reading like this.

Country people slept early - "Early to bed, early to rise, makes a man healthy and wise." so the saying goes!... But most of us studied until quite late. "Ah, Chung ken ken tuk su" (study diligently). My paternal grandmother always encouraged me! We had this one particular kerosene pressured lantern to light up our nights for reading. In some respect, we mankind did make some noteworthy progress. The pressured lantern is a bright lantern that can light up a large room. The pressured lantern we had was made of chrome-plated steel. It burned kerosene vapour (not liquid kerosene), so it had to be first preheated with a small flame. There was a small cup inside the lantern, which we filled with a teaspoon or so of alcohol. We would light this alcohol with a match. When the alcohol was about to finish burning, we would turn the fuel knob on, and the lantern would start to glow and light up. The lantern could produce brightness because it vaporized the kerosene and delivered the pressurized kerosene vapour to the mantle where it was burned (instead of burning liquid kerosene). When fully pumped, the kerosene pressured lantern could generate brightness as a few hundred-watt light bulbs we have today.

Early education

We walked to school. It was quite a distance for a young kid. On the way to school, we passed a river that wound its way downstream. This was the same river that passed in front of our house. But to me, this same river was more fast flowing at this stage downstream. I enjoyed walking to school with my little straw hat, which protected me from the tropical sun. The straw hat was light. One sweltering day, on our way home, I jumped into this river to cool myself off without realizing that I had on the little old straw hat. It fell off, and I tried hard to retrieve it. That was the last time I saw that straw hat!

Rays of sunlight came through the cracks of the wooden walls. I was inside a storeroom somewhere at Tai Tung School Sandakan. I was naughty, making too much noise and disturbing the class. In those days, we were not told to sit and face the wall. To not "spare the rod," so to speak, the teacher sent me in there, in this dark storeroom. I needed to pee. This storeroom was full of blue and white-coloured dishes. There was a huge vase almost as tall as me. Which smaller dish was better to pee into was not my priority. I was not choosy. I just wanted to relieve myself pronto. But in the end, I spared the dishes and decided to pee on the ground stead. When I was a law student in the early 1960s, I visited the British Museum of History in London and saw similar dishes and vases. I realized that those I came across in my early childhood in the storeroom at Tai Tung School were faked Ming wares.

During my visit to the Sacred Way and The Ming Tombs (2 weeks before the 2008 Beijing Summer Olympics), I came across a similar-looking vase, a specimen of the ancient Chinese handicraft. Of course, it would be heresy to say anything but in praise of such a magnificent work of art. But I was pretty disappointed and failed to see its merit, neither in its design nor the craft, despite what the tourist brochures said. Our tour guide elaborated on its magnificence, and most people around me exclaimed at its beauty. I have always thought that it might do us well if people simply hold their own views or ideas on whatever subject, instead of parrot-like, repeating others' opinions and sayings.

Christian life

By the time I was eight, I had started attending primary three at Sung Siew School. Sung Siew had its origin in 1907 as a Mission School for Chinese settlers. It was founded as a mission school by the Basel Mission Church and was known as the Basel Mission School. A few years later, the Basel Mission in Basel, Switzerland, sent a pastor as the school's first principal to start the English Section. The School was extensively destroyed during the Japanese invasion. The rectory built by the Mission was the only part of the structure left after the war. It was later renovated for occupation by the missionaries from the Lutheran Church of America. The Lutheran Church of America used to send their missionaries to do mission works and teach simultaneously. Sung Siew in Chinese means "twin educations." In Sung Siew School, one could choose to have English as the medium of instruction with Chinese as a second language. My father chose this line of education for us.

You could say I am a cradle Christian. I grew up in a household that went to church on Sunday and in which Christianity was practised. We went to Sunday service at the Basel Mission Church in Sandakan, and after church, dad would take us for a long drive on Labuk Road, all the way to mile thirteen. It was a treat to which I always looked forward. I joined the Basel Mission Choir as a child chorister. One evening in Advent, a long time ago, when I was perhaps 12 or 13 years old, we went out to sing carols at the home of the General Manager of Harrisons & Crossfield. Both my father and our Choir Master were the staff of this British trading company. The boss was entertaining guests at the Company's Christmas party. In the middle of our singing, my Choir Master quietly signaled me to stop singing. I was naturally hurt. It turned out that my voice was breaking as I was in transition from a child to a young adult (and eventually to manhood) - A Continuing Journey Of Belief And Faith – Pilgrimage. https://www.freepilgrim.com/a-continuing-journey-of-belief-and-faith/. Many of us children and young people were involved in church activities. Still, I have never experienced nor heard of the subject of concerns or allegations of abuse as widely portrayed in today's media.

In those days, priests customarily used to visit parishioners in their homes. One day, Pastor Johnson, the Lutheran priest and Principal of Sung Siew called on us in Sibuga. As he was walking up the wooden stairs of our house, the staircase creaked under his weight. I overheard him saying to my father, "On Tet, you are very blessed with so many children." I was thinking: How could we be? I could not even have my own basketball. Years later, it dawned on me that "blessings" could come in many forms, not just in material things. We need to look for them in all life situations. It is up to us to accept or deny them. Today I see the blessings in the fruits coming from my parents in the Fung Family Tree. I see the blessings at Christmases and weddings and whenever we, the descendants of Fung on Tet and Liew Nyuk Chin, gather. Others can be a blessing to us. In the Creation Story, God created the great sea creatures, the fish, and the birds and blessed them all. Blessings on us may come even from the animals, the birds, and even the plants around us.

As far back as I can remember, I have always been involved in the decorations for Christmas. Even though perhaps modest, we made every attempt to decorate for "the most wonderful time of the year" with whatever natural materials that looked attractive in the forest of Sibuga. We did not have winter "season" - just the Advent season. The festivity and spirit created by the approaching Christmas holiday season would lift our mood even though Santa never came to Sibuga. We did not have the tradition of gift-giving. But there would be a nice-looking branch of the merkus pine as our Christmas tree, decorated with bits of ribbon, paper strings, and homemade decorations. We would tie small candles to the branches and throw pieces of cotton wool all over that we pretended to be snow. Somehow all the Christmas cards we received had snowy scenes. I always dreamed of and wished for a White Christmas. I dreamed of waking up early in the morning, pretending and imagining that our ground there was covered by sparkling white snow.

Sung Siew School

Pastor Johnson, who was the school principal in the early fifties, was credited with constructing the first science laboratory in Sandakan. After school, together with other students, I helped him dig holes to prepare for the science room building foundation. We were excited when the science room was finally completed and equipped with microscopes, burners, and test tubes. In science class, my first surprise was looking through a microscope at some free-living freshwater amoebae found in the water we collected from puddles near the school. Though I enjoyed this thrilling part of biology, I was never going to make it as a scientist. Our Science laboratory attracted some students from other schools. Students from different schools interested in pursuing science sought the opportunity to be transferred to Sung Siew because of our science classes. By the time I graduated, Sung Siew had already sent many science-stream students to pursue further education in the medical, dental, and veterinary fields. Out of the three of us who graduated with Grade I Cambridge School Leaving Certificates (1960), one became a doctor and the other a dentist. I took up law instead.

The year was 1955. It was one of those years of James Dean. The years of "Rebel without a cause." We had a teacher from Ireland who always wore short pants. Sometimes he would prop one foot on his chair, and his cotton underpants would be visible underneath.

Sometimes he had no underwear. We controlled ourselves from laughing. Around that time, we also had a few teachers who were recruited from India. I think this teacher, Mr. Underwood was from Delhi and not Cochin. Between us students, we never referred to him as "Mr. Underwood." We always referred to him as "Indian teacher." This East Indian teacher was a very fussy person. He forever dashed himself with strong cologne. We had also observed that most of the time, he preferred to sit on the chair when he was teaching, rising only occasionally when he needed to write something on the blackboard. He did not use the blackboard often because he did not like chalk. The students (well, a few of us boys) ganged up and decided to do the trick on him. Someone had earlier come up with the idea that if we rub raw onions on his wooden chair, he would, after sitting on it for an extended period, start to fart.

"Quick, quick he is coming!" someone shouted as a warning. We quickly rubbed raw onions on his wooden chair. This trick seemed to work. He would periodically be farting very loudly in class. We could not control ourselves from giggling. Someone had also come up with the idea of using "Minyak Angin." The "Minyak Angin" is a powerful Chinese medicinal oil like Eucalyptus oil. We sprayed it all over the wooden walls of the classroom to counter his cologne. He would come into the classroom sniffing like an Alsatian. We would laugh and make so much noise and commotion in the classroom. We disrespected and insulted this teacher. He reported us to the principal. The few of us were suspended for a week by the school board. My dad was not mad with me, but neither did he spare the rod, so to speak. His rod was to demand that I draft a paper explaining the incidents. I have always wondered whether our naughty acts as teenagers deserved such severe punishment. Years later, I realized that even though no discipline or punishment of any kind felt good while being administered after that, the rewards were rich. I have tried to make that point to my children and others whenever I could.

"Sir, I need to go to the toilet." We found every excuse to ask permission to go to the toilet. The toilet of the school was a couple of hundred yards from our classroom. It was just a wooden shed divided into two sections, one for boys and one for girls. The hut was built on top of a vast pit dug out of the ground. Inside the shed was a hole through the wooden floor. It would be unwise to look down the hole. Unless we boys were desperate, we would not even go into the shed but preferred to pee in the bush nearby. Going to the loo was not really the reason to go. Just outside the toilet was a Chinese olive tree. Fruits were always in abundance on this tree because of the fertile (!) soil from which its roots obtained nutrients. We had no idea how far the roots extended. The tree belonged to the neighbour next to the school. He was frustrated with us climbing up his tree. He nailed pins all over the trunk to prevent us from climbing. Sung Siew school was also near a cemetery where a few star-fruit trees grew, and star fruits were always in abundance. The teachers were beginning to wonder why so many boys in our class needed to go to the toilets. And so often! We were in stages of puberty. I always wondered whether the teachers got the wrong idea.

The Dream

I finished school in 1960, blessed with a Grade One (1st Division) in the Senior Cambridge School Leaving Certificate (GCE) Examinations. I left for Jesselton (KK), hoping to see the Director of Education for a scholarship to pursue further education overseas. The name Jesselton was changed to Kota Kinabalu (KK) in 1963-after the famous mountain. My uncle pulled a string in the interim and got me a temporary teaching job in Lok Yuk School in Jesselton. The Basel Mission also ran Lok Yuk School. There was no need for us to qualify in those days to obtain a teaching certificate to teach. Many of us were "teachers" after we finished our Secondary education. While teaching at Lok Yuk School, I enrolled myself as an external student and ordered Constitutional Laws and Legal History from The University of London (External Exam for LLB). I used to sit on the spandex tin roof of my uncle's house in his small rubber estate in KK while I read the papers sent to me by the University. This roof was also the spot at which I did my vocal exercise.

Pastor Nelson, my mentor at Basel Mission in Jesselton, tried to persuade me to enter the seminary to become a priest. Unfortunately, I did not have the Calling. I was determined to be a lawyer. Somehow, I knew I had to. With my favourable GCE performance, I was told and was confident that I qualified for the Colombo Plan Scholarship. However, Mr. Muir, the Director of education, had turned me down for a scholarship to study law for reasons only known to himself. My uncle noticed that I wanted very much to pursue further education. He convinced my dad to give me the opportunity. So, my father had to mortgage his land for a loan to finance me to go to England to pursue my dream.

The Voyage

Encounters on SS. Kajang

"Good evening, Judge." His Lordship was sailing SS. Kajang from KK to Singapore. Where he was heading to, after Singapore, I had not the faintest idea. He was traveling with his wife, and they were on the same vessel with me, except they were in the First-Class cabin. I was bunking in a cabin a couple of decks below, near the ship's engine. I shared the cabin with a lady and her teenage daughter, also bound for Singapore. I ran into the Judge and his gracious wife by chance on the open main deck as they were strolling and watching the golden sun setting behind Gaya Island. I knew he was a Judge, and I had learned how to address a High Court Judge by the time left for England. His Lordship just said "Hello," but his wife, surprised by my salutation, asked me where I was going. I told them I was on my way to England to read Law and that I had been accepted by the Honourable Society of The Inner Temple. The Inner Temple is one of the prestigious four Inns of Court (professional associations for barristers and judges) located in the wider Temple area near the Royal Courts of Justice, in London. The Inn provides legal training, selection, and regulation for members. Both the judge and his wife looked impressed. After a few casual exchanges, they wished me Godspeed.

The Vessel

The ship "Chitral" of the P & O Shipping Line.

I do not know why my father decided to send me to England by sea. The vessel was "Chitral" of the world-renowned P & O Line sailing from Singapore through the Suez Canal to England. The Chitral was a small ship bought by P& O from Belgium. I learned later that she was scrapped in Taiwan in 1975. I had a cabin below the main deck with four bunks to myself. I chose to sleep in the same top bunk for the whole journey because I did not know whether they allowed me to sleep in the others. My cabin was quite close to the engine room. The trip would take us a total of 21 days from Singapore to London. I was seated, mealtime with an elderly Chinese couple who were noticeably quiet. We had the same European menus as the rest of the British and American passengers. The headwaiter must have observed us. One evening he asked whether I would like to be seated with some of the boys on board. I accepted without hesitation.

New friends

The Purser of the Ship reallocated my seating for meals. They moved me to join Peter, Nigel, and Blakey. These boys were VSOs (volunteers service overseas) returning to the motherland. They had just finished their services overseas after their services in South East Asia. "I am Peter," a young man with unkempt short blond hair and an Oxford accent stretched out his hand to shake mine. He must have sensed that I was shy and feeling a bit uncertain of myself. I knew Queen's English when I heard one. It sounded so much like the way Her Majesty spoke over the radio. After serving as a VSO teacher in Tenom, where he spent more than a year, Peter returned to England. I told him I knew a girl Katherine Hurst, a VSO who taught at Sabah College. That broke the ice. Peter and I became friends. That was in 1963.

Even though I was sitting with these boys, I still had the same European cuisine. The food was foreign and strange to my Chinese palate, coming straight from Sibuga. Again, the observant headwaiter must have noticed and reported to the Purser. He told me to see the purser. The purser asked me whether I would like to have the food they cooked for the Chinese crew on board. I accepted. The meal was simple but tasty. I found out later that Peter was bunking with these two other VSOs in a cabin a few doors down the corridor from mine. I would learn to play bridge with the boys. From then onwards, we were a perfect foursome for bridge, our primary pass time, for the sea's long journey.

When I was serving as the Attorney-General years later, I invited Peter and his wife Janine to Sabah to give him the thrill of walking down memory lane. I took them to Keningau, Tenom, Kundasang, Mount Kinabalu National Park, and the Hot Springs near Ranau, where we took nothing but photos and left behind only our footprints. They were staying with us at our home on Signal Hill. Often, in the evenings, we would walk on the sandy beach of Tanjung Aru, a place which had long afforded me comfort while stressed with my complicated life. "Rollers on the beach, wind in the pines...drown out the hectic rhythms of city and suburbs, timetables and schedules" - Anne Morrow Lindbergh wrote in her book *gift from the sea*. Peter and Janine stayed with us for several weeks, and I believe they both had enjoyed the visit to Sabah. When my family and I were in England on vacation in 2007, we visited them in Kent. They drove from Folkstone, Kent, to meet us after our Sunday service at Canterbury Cathedral and took us back to their home for lunch. It was nice to have caught up with each other again after more than forty years.

On our way to Colombo on board Chitral, we passed through this part of the ocean, not what fishermen would call a lively ground. I was sitting on a deck chair by the pool and looking beyond the horizon. "Can you put this on my back, please? "an American woman asked me rhetorically while showing me a bottle of suntan lotion in her right hand and stretching it towards me. I knew she was American because I had heard Ava Gardner, Lana Turner, Rita Hayworth, Susan Hayward, and Marilyn Monroe spoke in movies. The woman sounded more like Rita Hayworth. I obliged her but also said to her that she could get severely burned in this tropical sun. She seemed disappointed at my comment. I saw her repeatedly around the swimming pool, but she just smiled and never asked me again to help with the suntan lotion.

When not playing bridge with the boys, I would be spending time reading the Papers I had ordered from the University of London. I would usually read in my cabin but sometimes also on deck. One day I was watching an American family from Texas playing deck tennis. They saw me watching them playing and invited me to join them. I learned the game quickly and began to enjoy playing it, especially with his daughter, a pretty girl in her late teens. She reminded me of my American pen pal from Minnesota, but prettier. I mentioned to her about Jo Ellen, who had been my pen pal for several years when I was at Sung Siew School. I got Jo Ellen's contact from Pastor Dugan, who was our Principal at the time. I still have a photo of Jo Ellen, but I am a bit sad that I no longer remember the name of the girl I had played deck tennis with on the ship.

The Egyptian Pyramids 1963

The Sphinx Egypt 1963

We sailed through the Suez Canal into Port Said. When the ship docked, we could see Arab traders going about their trades. There were no signs left of Operation Musketeer, and Operation Kadesh

33

carried out a few years before. The American family and I went to see the Sphinx. The American girl, her younger brother, and I entered the Pyramid of Khufu through what appeared to me dark tunnels. We were trying to reach the inner chamber under this massive stone pyramid through these dark and circuitous tunnels. We managed to get to what we thought was the centre of the pyramid and discovered it was just an empty chamber. Did I expect to find treasures of some kind? How could it be otherwise, knowing this was the inside chamber where the Pharaoh lay in state buried with his possessions. But the reality never did live up to my fantasy. In 2009 while doing the "Steps of Paul," I mentioned this incident to my driver. The driver, originally from Algeria, told me that a person who had entered the pyramids would live a long life. Who knows?

The storm

As Chitral approached Gibraltar in 1963

Leaving Port Said, the journey sailing through the Mediterranean was not what I had expected. The sea was rough, particularly at night.

34

Many of the passengers got seasick—two of my bridge partners among them. I had learned that the sea's stretch, including The Bay of Biscay, off the west coast of France and north of Spain, tend to be roughest in the Autumn and winter due to the winds and storms. I knew that we might encounter rough sailings from time to time, but I never knew the offender would be the Mediterranean. A voice came over the ship's microphone, informing us that we would be docking at Gibraltar soon. This morning, the Rock, through the mist and a relatively calmer sea, could be seen from a distance. Upon arrival, we instantly noticed the distinctive British Flares because it was owned by the British. Gibraltar was the port I had to say goodbye to the American family. They were getting off here to go over to Spain and to tour part of Europe. Many of the other passengers also disembarked for the day trip.

Inside the Cave in Gibraltar

Peter and I explored Gibraltar on foot, ending up inside a cave where we saw those huge canons strategically mounted by the British to protect the Mediterranean Sea entrance. This Rock was one of History's most contested real estate pieces stretching a length of three miles and was brought under British control after British troops stormed it during the Spanish Succession War. It was ceded to Britain under the Treaty of Utrecht in perpetuity. Gibraltar had been an important base for the British and, at the time of our arrival, Britain's Naval base. On the way back to our ship Peter and I played with the delightful tailless monkeys which roamed the Rock. After we embarked on the Ship that evening, the weather changed on us for the worse. The rest of the journey was truly unpleasant. There were fewer people at the dining tables in the evenings because most of them were seasick. I was not feeling too good either, and the food was tasteless.

Everyone was relieved when we finally reached Britain and Chitral entered the Thames Estuary. I was now sailing on this famous river that I have read so much about in literary works. I had read that the River was tidal in London with a rise and fall of 23 feet and was non-tidal at Eddington Lock. However, it was nighttime, and I was unable to see much. By the time I woke up, we were already approaching the east end of London. On this last day of our trip, I saw what appeared to me to be many warehouses and factories. "Are your parents coming to meet you?" I asked Peter. "I hope so; they haven't seen me for more than a year," he muttered, with a wee bit of anxiousness. I felt lonely although I knew Mr. Longfield of the British Council had planned for someone to receive me on arrival and take me to the British Council's office, which would then sort out temporary accommodation for me.

It was a foggy morning. The ship finally docked. Through the fog, Peter was delighted to see his parents, who waved at him from the dock. In those days, people could come on board to meet passengers. So, they came on board, and his mother kissed him on the cheeks. Peter shook hands with his dad, and he introduced me to them. His mother commented that Peter had lost a lot of weight. They knew that a British Council representative would be here to meet me and waited with me. The British Council representative eventually found me. Peter's parents invited me to come to their house as soon as possible after settling down.

The British Council

The British Council representative took me in a London taxi to their office near the Oxford Circus underground station. "How do you find London?" he asked me in the cab. I did not know how to answer. "Oh, I just noticed lots of warehouses and factories," I replied, not knowing whether the answer was polite and proper. In my mind, I thought England, so far, was the foggiest country I have ever seen. I had been reading "Do and don't," but the little book never covered this area of etiquette. I left it at that.

I sat outside Mr. Longfield's office and waited for him. A girl came and asked me to go in, and I followed her. Mr. Longfield's office was not a particularly big one. It was smaller than I envisaged. He had a typical working desk, and there were two chairs for his visitors. He gestured for me to sit down. His room was smoky. He looked through my file and asked me a few questions, and gave some advice. He then told me to see someone in the general office outside who would help me with my London accommodation. A girl in the general office beckoned me and asked me to sit down. She told me that The British Council would provide me with one-week accommodation. In the interim, I had to look for one to rent for a more extended stay. She also told me where they were putting me up for the week. Then she showed me and gave me a list of full board and half board accommodations approved by the British Council for overseas students.

I was given maps to the London Underground, which they called the Tube. The Oxford Circus was a convenient station. The place they were putting me up for a week was at Gloucester Road. Someone from the office would take me there later. I would have to be on my own after that. My accommodation for the week at Gloucester Road was a room on the second floor in a small hotel. It was a luxury to me because it had a long bath. I had never been in a tub like this in all my life. In fact, I never had, except in movies, seen one like it. I washed my face, freshened up, and decided to explore. There were very few restaurants and shops in the surrounding area.

There was a small Chinese takeout, selling noodles and rice. I saw roast chickens through the glass window of a shop nearby. I bought a roast chicken and a loaf of bread from this shop run by someone who spoke to his employees in a language I could not understand. They also had this enormous chunk of meat standing vertically and rotating around a roaster in the shop. A couple of days later, I ordered this dish. The seller sliced the meat from the large chunk, added some sliced lettuce, and wrapped it up with a thin pancake. It tasted perfect and became one of my regular takeouts. Many years later, the Doner Kebab was again one of my typical food when I, on my journey as Free Pilgrim, was trying to trace the footsteps of St. Paul in Turkey.

Lodgings in London

21 Old Oak Road

I desperately looked for "digs" to rent (within my monthly budget of 40 Sterling Pounds). While on the train on the District Line from South Kensington to the Inner Temple, I noticed a small advertisement in the Evening Standard regarding a room for rent to students. In answer to this ad, I went and knocked on the door. An older woman with short blond hair appeared. She looked at me and said: "We don't take in Chinese," at which point she closed the door. A knife pierced through my heart, a young man who had just left his home in Borneo for the first time in his simple life. I went into the Temple Church to seek solace. That evening I took another look at the list of accommodations given to me by the girl at the British Council Office. I found one that fitted my budget. It was an attic room at 21 Old Oak Road, Shepherd Bush. So, after a week under the British Council's aegis, I moved into this attic room. This room would remain as my residence for more than a year until Michael and his wife Mary from Singapore asked me to join them in sharing a flat at 48 Clonmel Road in Parsons Green.

Two elderly sisters owned 21 Old Oak Road. The older sister was frail and small compared to the younger sister, stout and heavy-looking. The older sister did the cooking, and the younger one ran the house and did all the housekeeping chores. The house had four rooms for rent to students, either at full or half board. The other boarders were a girl student from Nigeria, a boy from Pakistan, and a graduate medical student from Hong Kong. The house was not centrally heated, but there was a little gas fireplace with a coin slot for me to feed in guineas. I had to pay for the gas fire. The room was spartan, devoid of any decorations but otherwise reasonably comfortable. I had a single bed, one sitting chair, a writing table to put my books on, and a desk chair. I had a radio, which also acted as an alarm clock. One day I went to a small appliance shop in Shepherd Bush and bought myself a small electrical ring heater. I used it at night and stored it in the cupboard when not in use during the day. My landlady noticed the increase in electricity consumption when her electricity bill arrived. She searched the whole house and found the small electric ring heater in the cupboard in my room. She told me not to use it again because the rent did not cover electricity consumption.

Reading at 21 Old Oak Road Shepherd Bush England

One evening, few days after I had moved in, she came to the attic room. She turned down the bed and explained that I had to sleep between the top sheet and the bottom sheet. When she made the beds in the morning, she must have noticed that I had been sleeping on top for days and used the bed cover (eiderdown) as my blanket. It dawned on me that I had also never tucked myself between the top and bottom sheets when I was sailing on Chitral from Singapore to London. I was a simple Kampong boy from Borneo who, before this day, had slept only on the vinyl sheet with a blanket nearby, which I hardly used, except on an unusually chilly night in Sibuga. What did I know...?

I opted to stay half-board with my landladies because I would be away the entire day at Inner Temple. Chancery Lane, the tube station nearest to Inner Temple, was quite a way from Shepherds Bush. I discovered later that the White City station and not Shepherds Bush station on the Central line was nearer to where I lived. However, I came to know an old lady at the fruit stand in shepherd Bush station. "What can I do for you today, luve" she always greeted me like that. That was the way she pronounced "love." She was kind and always gave me a good deal for the apples I wanted to buy. So, on the day I wanted to buy some fruits, I would still choose to get off at Shepherd Bush station on my way back from Chancery Lane. I usually lunch at the students' Common Room, where they regularly served cole-slaw, baked beans on toast, fried eggs, spaghetti Bolognese, and fish and chips. Chips were always available as an item by themselves. Our dinner served by the two landladies consisted of minestrone, chicken, boiled Brussel sprouts, baked or mashed potatoes, and ice cream. If we were lucky or they were in a good mood, we got apple pie or a piece of cake for desserts - no guarantee - the rent did not cover these.

21 Old Oak Road under renovation 2007

I came to know this fellow boarder Dr. Hahn, a graduate medical student from Hong Kong who was doing a Radiology program at Hammersmith Hospital. I also came to know a final-year law student of Lincoln's Inn from Sibu, Sarawak, who lived a couple of houses away. Our landladies rested on weekends. Our rent did not cover meals for weekends. In any case, I missed Asian food, and going out, or a good takeout would be a welcome change. Fortunately, I had these two Chinese friends who would be my regular weekend companions at the local Chinese or Indian restaurants.

21 Old Oak Road in 2018

One night, BBC, which I always tuned into, made a Breaking News announcement: "President Kennedy has been shot!" John Fitzgerald Kennedy, the 35th President of the United States of America, was a hero of my pen pal Jo Ellen. She wrote to me about JFK. I first learned of JFK as a candidate for the Presidency from her while I was still in my final years at Sung Siew Secondary School. The picture of me standing, listening to the news, had been etched in my mind. Yes, even those immortal words: "Ask not what your country can do for you, ask what you can do for your country." I walked down memory lane in 2007 with May and our son Nigel and saw that someone had bought the house and in the process of renovating it. In the Autumn of 2018, May and I went there again and had a look at the attic room from Old Oak Road. After more than 50 years, I still have a vivid memory of that incredibly sad moment.

48 Clonmel Road

In the summer of 1964, Mary and Michael, whom I got to know through Dr. Hahn, asked me whether I would like to share a flat with them. They sent me to look for flats because they were both working. I looked at a few in different locations but ended up with the upper floor of 48 Clonmel Road, a short walk from Parson Greens Station. I would have liked to have rented a place near the City, but we could not afford the rent. Here, during weekends Michael and Mary would have friends coming over to play mahjong until the wee hours of the morning. One of their friends by the name of Klondike reminded me of Bruce Lee.

At 48 Clonmel Rd. Parsons Green 1966

"Frankie Frankie and Maggie" was a sign hanging at the door to the flat downstairs. Living on the lower floor of 48 Clonmel Rd. were two slim redhead Irish girls with the same name "Frances." and a plum English girl called Maggie. Maggie was originally from Bromley, a large town in southeastern Greater London. One of the Frankies moved out not long afterward, and the share of the tenancy was immediately taken up by Sally, a fair English girl with rosy cheeks. The remaining

Frankie had a boyfriend who came to visit her very often. He looked like Tom Jones with natural dark curly hair, which I envied. He looked in his late twenty, well built, rather tall, with dark eyes and lips ready for any girl. But what is this thing with fair-skinned women who like to suntan till their skin turns brown? Frankie was one of them. She would always ask me to help her apply suntan lotion on her back when she was about to go out to tan herself in the backyard. After the summer of 1965, she also moved out. Then one day, I ran into her by chance at Marble Arch Station. Her tan was gone, and she looked worn down with shallow cheek and a freckled face. We chatted on the platform for a while. Then the next train arrived, she stepped in, the door closed.

Frankie disappeared among the passengers in the crowded train. She was out of sight. That was the last time I saw her. Maggie had a boyfriend, with a lean and hungry look, by the name of Clive. He spoke with a strong East London cockney accent. Sally surprisingly had no boyfriend. One day we had a party, and there were some boys from Malaysia. I think Sally connected with a Chinese boy from Sarawak. This chap was a jovial fellow who laughed a good deal at other people's jokes and witticisms, making him extremely popular. I have no idea whether the relationship between him and Sally had worked out and lasted.

Parsons Green 2017

A lot has changed over the years in this once upon a time family-oriented neighbourhood of Parsons Green. On 15 September 2017, there was an explosion on the train at Parsons Green Station. Thirty people were injured by a botched, crude "bucket bomb" with a timer containing the TATP explosive chemical, and the police arrested the main suspect, an 18-year-old Iraqi asylum seeker. Europol classified the incident as a case of Jihadist terrorism. I was in London around that time. A few days after the attack, compassion and nostalgia impelled me to revisit this neigbourhood. But on my journey to this southern suburb of London, I was pleasantly surprised to see men, women, and children going about their usual way of life despite the nameless and unjustified terror which paralyzed this area a few days before. But "Why Parsons Green?" We pondered...

The Doultons

"Good Morning, Mrs. Doulton," I greeted Daphne Doulton, Peter's mother, as she opened the door of her house to welcome me. I handed her a bouquet of local flowers, which I picked up from Shepherd Bush station. Peter lived with his parents and four other siblings, two older brothers, one younger brother, and one younger sister. Peter's dad, Alfred Doulton, was the Headmaster of Highgate School. Peter had given me instructions for directions to their house just before I left my dig that morning. Peter had told me to get off at East Finchley Station. From there, it was a short walk. The Doulton's residence was a three-story end unit of a school Block. It was an enormous building in Highgate High School's compound close to the Highgate Golf Club and Hampstead Heath. Hampstead was the most desirable residential real estate in London. Inside the residence block, there was everything that I never had.

At Christmas Lunch at the Doultons

They had a long dining table in the dining room, a grand piano in the sitting room, a full-size Billiard table, and even a darkroom for photography in the basement. The Doultons invited me to stay with them for two weeks every Christmas holiday when I was in London as a Law Student. Sometimes, we had Christmas lunches with international students from High Gate High school and the Doultons' relatives. I also joined the family for Christmas Eve services at their local church. The boys and I sang carols in the neighbourhood. We went around pub-crawling to raise funds for OXFAM. I even tried a Gaelic folk dance. I remember it was a dance that consisted of a sequence of figures. A group of us would be dancing and tracing some progressive steps and patterns. Alfred and Daphne Doulton were an amazing couple. They were kind and gracious. I still have a mental picture of hundreds and hundreds of Christmas cards hanging on their walls every Christmas. Years later, Peter's father retired to Salcombe in Devon, where he passed on. When I was still in Sabah Bank, Peter wrote to me. He told me that when his father died, he noted that many people had to stand outside the church at his memorial service because the parish church was not big enough to accommodate them.

Summer Breaks

The Hunt was so aristocratic and the riders so elegant with their riding gears. However, Fox Hunting has since been banned in England by the Hunting Act 2004. Horses had always fascinated me, perhaps because I am a Centaur born in the Year of the Horse. I wanted to learn to ride a horse. I read in The Evening Standard about a riding school in Wimbledon. In 1964, I made my way from Parson Green to Wimbledon Common and Richmond Park, hoping to find a riding instructor willing to teach me. I had no money for the riding lesson but readied to work at the stable. I met the owner of a riding school by the name of Somosky. "Sir, I want to learn how to ride." He looked at me and asked me whether I was a student. I told him that I was. I asked him how much my fees would be. "We can work out something," he said. He was a decent specimen of humanity.

Horsing riding at Richmond Park England

He told me that he was a retired Polish Cavalry captain. After that, I always addressed him as "Captain Somosky." He said, "Ok, let's try." He gave me brief instructions on how to mount the horse, helped me with my left foot into the stirrup, and pushed my right leg up and over the horse's back to the stirrup on the right. I walked the horse, and somehow it broke into a trot, and I was bumping up and down relatively uncoordinated. After a while, I managed to get into the trot's rhythm. I started to rise and down in tandem with the trot's movements. He told me to dismount and said I could come back next Tuesday. He probably noticed that I was athletic and with good coordination. The following Tuesday, I joined a group of six riders. We learned to trot and canter. I had an obedient mount. I learned to pull the rein gently on the left and nudge him with my right heel, and he would lead with his front right.

By the third lesson, Captain Somosky saw that I had improved on coordination and balance in all three gaits. He instructed me to join the group of experienced riders to jump over a stream. This stream was relatively shallow, with grass on both banks. It was about 4 -5 feet wide with truly little water in it because it was summer. We jumped by turn. All six of the horses had jumped over. They were on the other side about a hundred yards away, and it was my turn. My horse broke from a trot into a canter - faster and faster. We reached the stream, and I was ready to jump him. He stopped abruptly. The momentum of the canter took me with it. I fell forward over his head into the stream but was not hurt except for my ego. I got out of the stream and remounted.

"Try again. This time give him slack and lean forward before the jump." Captain Somosky instructed. The others were watching with interest from across on the other side. I took a big turn and started to canter the horse once again towards the stream. I got ready, flexed my knees, and leaned a bit forward just before the jump. I gave him confidence. He sensed it, and over the stream, he jumped, and we landed on the other side. I heard the applause. I was thrilled. "I am a natural," I thought to myself. I gently patted the neck of my horse with my right hand. He was not particularly huge, a lovely 14 hands 2 inches Bay Gelding. We were now a team. Unfortunately, I have forgotten his name.

I never had to pay for my lessons. Captain Somosky gave me a job. He had two stables. After the lessons, I unbridled and removed the saddles and stored all the riding gears. I was to clean and groom the horses. One day he told me to come early, ride my horse to the other stable, and bring over three other horses. The other stable had six box stalls, and in one of them, there was a big pile of hay. There were two stable girls. They took care of the horses, the feeds, the hay and kept the stables in good condition. One of the girls was quite pretty, and she was friendly. She looked at me briefly. The glance of her blue eyes was uncomfortably direct. "Are you a student?" she asked me with a strong cockney accent. I answered her "yes" softly while dusting an invisible speck of dust from my riding jacket. Her name was Rose...a common pleasant name I thought and easy to remember. We carried on a casual conversation as I continued saddling the horses and adjusting the stirrups. She told me it was her summer job, and she was from Cheapside East London. The name of that place sounded familiar. I had flashes of Ms. Innis, my favourite teacher in English literature, reciting Shakespeare, or maybe I read it in Jane Austin's Pride and Prejudice. The other girl was busy forking the hay from one stall to the next.

The reins and bridles were now in place. I mounted my horse, and Rose led the other three horses and passed me the reins. I had a good look at her since she was now out of the stable and in full sight. Not only was she pretty, but she also had a great figure which she presumably got from her physical exercises. Even with her low-rise pull-on knee patched breeches, I could tell she had lovely legs, which no one could ignore. I thought she was nice, but I was not sure how good a stable hand she made for Captain Somosky. I left her at that but had hope of returning to this stable again one day. Leading the horses with the reins in one hand, I trotted over to the school where Captain Somosky was waiting with the other students.

I managed to develop the finesses of riding a horse to the next level. I learned to have deeper seating and more effective use of the aids. I was now riding a different horse and learned dressage, and Captain Somosky started us with the pole work and then the grid. I went all the way up to the novice show jump. However, the incredible thrill I had in those summer days was when he took us into Richmond Park and told us to ride bareback without saddle and reins. We were riding without aids, holding on to the horse's mane and gripping the horse with our knees. We even managed to jump over the enormous trunks of some fallen trees. On one occasion, while my horse was trotting briskly among the trees and I was looking out for low branches to duck under, one of the other six horses just stood there eating grass and refusing to move. I worked in the summers for Captain Somosky until my Bar Finals, when I had to concentrate on the Law entirely. Altogether I had 24 complete riding lessons with him of one hour each and learned all I could in the limited period. I never saw Captain Somosky again. When I tried to look him up many years later, I was told that he had already passed on. I will always remember this nice man who allowed me to learn to ride, and I will never forget those summer days I spent with him...

Other interests.

"All work and no play make Jack a dull boy," I was told many times by my landlady when she saw me so engrossed over the law books. For the first six months after I arrived in London, I had no friends. The books, not just law books, in the attic, were my friends. Someone had given me a King James Bible. I cannot remember who gave it to me. I would occasionally open to the Old Testament. I read the stories of adventure, journeys, and greatness of the prophets that weave through the Old Testament pages. And when I reached the verses which interested me, I would read slowly and sometimes linger - the stories of Abraham, Jacob, Noah, and God speaking to Moses in the burning bush... I would linger where God chose to speak with His people...

There were days I had cooped myself up in this tiny room for hours. The Trinity Term of 1964 was over. I should take the advice of my landlady. One late afternoon I had the urge to go to learn ice-skating. I took the Central Line and got off at Queensway Station. I walked to the Queensway Ice-Skating Rink, rented a pair of skates, and went on to the rink. It was very slippery. I hang on carefully to the side of the rink even though my balance was good because I did roll-skating at Sung Siew School. I remember we used to roller-skate down the hill, all the way to my "auntie's" house.

I was sure ice-skating would be a breeze for me. I gathered my confidence and glided across the rink to the other side, although we were supposed to skate around the rink anti-clockwise. One of the girls skating there must have been observing me. She slid towards me and bumped into me as if by accident. "Sorry," she apologized. "Hello, it's ok," I said, secretly thinking I was happy to be bumped. She was only sixteen years old and came to the rink with her father and her younger brother. Her name was Josephine. I later learned that the father was a frigate commander in the Royal Navy based in Penang before Malaysia Day. They had lived in Malaya and Singapore for several years. She told me she was brought up by a nanny dressed in white but had long black hair that she bundled up and secured with a jaw claw clip - such a memory of her childhood, I thought.

Josephine's father, Commander Fletcher, had already been posted back to England for two years when I met him. He was now an Admiralty Officer at the War Office in Whitehall, London. The family lived on a houseboat in Chiswick West London. He invited me to come up to his house if I wanted. "You can always help me with repainting the houseboat," he said. Jokingly perhaps, but I found out later that he did have a sense of humour. It was already late summer, and the holiday would soon be over. I managed to get to their house only twice, the first time was after Josephine and I had gone out to see the show "Nutcrackers" specially staged for students. We had previously arranged to meet at Fulham Station from where we would take the Tube to Covent Garden for the London Opera House. Her mother drove her to Fulham Station. "Be good," the mom said. "Yes, Mrs. Fletcher." I politely responded. After all, Josephine was 16 years old, and I felt like an old man at 21 and a half.

The summer holiday was over, and Josephine went back to her private boarding school in Reading. We corresponded for a few months and then lost touch. I do not remember how or why it ended. There is a saying that the bowl of water closest to the moon gets her image first. But this reminded me of one of my favourite Paul Anka's single written and released in 1960. Were we "puppies"? In the meantime, I continued to skate at the Queensway Skating Rink. One evening I tried the One Foot Upright Spin, broke my right ankle, felt, and sat on the ice. I could not move. It was strange that I did not feel much pain. The emergency staff called for an ambulance. Paramedics came. They slowly and carefully loaded me onto a stretcher and took me to the Hammersmith Hospital, where the doctor attended to my fractures. My right lower leg remained plaster cast for more than six weeks. I had to walk with crutches when I could do so. It was so itchy when it started to heal. It was torture because I could not reach the area to scratch it with the plaster in place. I found and cut a section of a wire cloth hanger, bent it, and used it to reach the itchy part of my leg. That was a relief! In consequence of this accident, my right foot is slightly shorter than my left and the right bony knob, called the lateral malleolus, which I can still feel at the outside, is larger than the one on my left. Life goes on...

Legal Education

At Inner Temple Law Library

I had made an appointment to see the Sub-Treasurer of Inner Temple. The Sub-Treasurer was the Chief Executive responsible for and regularly reported all aspects of the Inn's activities. I called at his office situated on the building's ground floor, which housed the Inner Temple Law Library. The secretary Ana Marie indicated to me that I could go in. Commander Rodney Fynn (RN), Sub-Treasurer of the Inner Temple, was sitting behind his desk by the large windows which overlooked the Temple Garden. There were several paintings with ornate wooden frames hanging on the wall opposite. One of the pictures depicted riders and horses in a foxhunting scene. He got up, a little heavily, to shake my hand. I could see that he was a stout man with a big belly and a classic handlebar mustache turning to grey. He went back to his seat and told me to sit down on one of the padded wooden chairs in front of his desk. He casually asked why I had chosen Inner Temple. That was my first test at the Inn; at least, that was how I felt. "You will have to sit for the required numbers of dinners," Commander Flynn reminded me. He sounded like an old master. "Yes, Sir," I responded without thinking.

The Inner Temple is one of the four Inns of Court (the others are Middle Temple, Gray's Inn, and Lincoln's Inn), which hold the exclusive right to call candidates to practise law at the Bar of England and Wales. To gain access to most other professions passing an examination or two was enough. But for a call to the Bar in England and Wales is different: qualification as a Barrister-at-law is contingent on law graduates attending a dozen formal dinners. I discovered that May was the dining season's height for the Dining Hall of the Inner and Middle Temple. Dozens of hopefuls tried to cram in enough meals to enable them to be "called to the Bar" upon completion of their studies and passing all their Bar Examinations. I noticed prospective young barristers in the dining dress code of dark colour suits and black gowns en route to the dining hall after their lectures. Black gowns were provided at the entrance to the dining hall if students were not wearing one.

Law students at Inner Temple 1964

We loaded ourselves on sumptuous and subsidized food served by waiters on long dining tables. There was good red and white wine, one bottle each placed in the middle of the table in front of four diners. The wine was an endowment by some philanthropist members of the Inns. This ritual has its roots all the way back to the time when the Temples were responsible for vocational legal education. The sons of country gentlemen would come to lodge at the Inns, attend lectures, and participate in mock court trials. The students and barristers would dine together in the fraternity in the main halls of the Inns. Things have changed over the years. During my time, the Council of Legal Education conducted barristers' professional training, but the dinners live on...

The Inner Temple was a distinct society from at least 1388, although its founding's precise date is unknown as with all the Inns of Court. The Temple has been closely linked to Magna Carta and its legacy ever since 1214. "The Temple was King John's London headquarters (1214-15). From here, he issued two vital preliminary charters, and here in January 1215, the barons confronted him for the first time with the demand that he subjects himself to the rule of a charter."- Robin Griffith-Jones, DLitt, The Reverend and Valiant Master of the Temple.

The Temple has also been linked with the United States of America ever since. Lawyers from The Temple drew up the early American colonies' constitutions; five signed the Declaration of Independence and seven the American Constitution. The Magna Carta (or Great Charter) informs Canada's legal system and the Canadian Charter of Rights and Freedom. The agreement between King John of England and his barons provided the English common law's foundation, which spread throughout the English-speaking world.

Besides spending my time at the Inner Temple Law Library, I spent a lot of time at the Temple Church situated between the Middle and

Inner Temple. The Knights Templars constructed the Church, an Order (of crusading monks) founded in the 12th century to protect pilgrims on their way to and from Jerusalem. After the Order was abolished in 1312, lawyers at the Temple site eventually formed themselves into two societies, the Inner Temple and Middle Temple, which was first mentioned in the manuscript yearbook of 1388. The historical record shows that since 1608 The Temple has been the collegiate Church of Inner and Middle Temple's legal colleges. The Church is in two parts: The Round and the Chancel. It was designed to recall the circular Church of the Holy Sepulchre in Jerusalem. The Round Church was consecrated in 1185 by the Patriarch of Jerusalem - http://www.freepilgrim.com/journey-back-in-time/

The Temple Church England

I started Michaelmas Term in 1963. By Hilary Term 1966, I had managed to pass all the required Examinations for the call to the Bar. I had my last dinner sometime in May 1966. Someone had to sponsor a student for the call to the Bar. I was now ready to be called, but I needed to find a sponsor. I knew a Master of the Bench - Bencher Neville Jonas Laski QC. He was a regular at the Inner Temple Law Library, where I also spent a considerable amount of time. Master Laski was a Barrister and was appointed a King's Counsel (KC) before I was even born. He was a deeply learned man who was already made a Bencher of the Inner Temple in 1930. Master Laski was a Judge of Appeal of the Isle of Man. I believed he knew me as a student reading law daily at the Library. He was prepared to be my sponsor. I still have a mental picture of him walking past me at my reading desk in the Inner Temple Law Library. "Golden lads and girls all must, As chimney-sweepers, come to dust." - William Shakespeare. The inevitable happened. He passed away a few years after my Call. I will remember him and have always been grateful for his sponsorship.

The Swinging Sixties

The cultural revolution was taking place in the 1960s. It was not just the Cultural Revolution launched in China by communist leader Mao Zedong to reassert his authority over the Chinese government. In the West, it was the swinging sixties. The sixties would introduce all the countries concerned (including England) everything from different rock music, rampant drug use, tattooing, profanity, hippies, and feminism. Free love was commonplace. The Beatles were becoming a global sensation even though I did not take to their music. My preference remained jazz, easy listening by Sinatra, Nat King Cole, and Matt Monroe. I came to know few law students from Sabah and Sarawak. The students from Sarawak mainly were children of wealthy parents. One of them from Kuching partied a lot. One night he invited me to a party in his flat.

I still remember he had a massive bowl of punch he said was a mix of vodka and orange juice. It was a huge punch bowl with a ladle in it and crystal glasses by the side. I saw slices of oranges floating in the punch, but the punch was more vodka than orange juice. I picked up one of the crystal glasses and admired its beauty. I helped myself with half a glass of the punch, at first...He also had many bottles of Younger's Bitter beer and Guinness Stouts on the table by the corner of his living room. There were many vibrant and bubbly girls among his guests. I drank too much that night. The following day, I had my first experience of a hangover. He invited me again, but I politely declined. I found out many years later that he never graduated.

At Lake Districts England

I bought secondhand or used jackets. The word "preowned" did not exist. The dynamic social changes sweeping the world would soon also manifest themselves in fashion. Before the so-called British Invasion in 1964, the fashion was a continuation of the late 1950s, conservative and restrained, classic in style and design. Then the Beatles appeared on the scene. With the Beatles came a new and hugely different kind of fashion, influenced not by Paris or Milan but by "swinging" London and Liverpool. New freedom in hemlines, a bolder approach to colours, bright and psychedelic. Fashion would parallel the youth movement, yearning for choices that did not mimic their preceding generations. Women were liberating themselves from the uncomfortable and matronly attire of the fifties. Armed with synthetic materials came new female clothing lines. The miniskirts and hot pants were ready to explode onto the market. 1960s Fashion - Styles that trended in the 1960s. https://fiftiesweb.com/fashion/1960s-fashion/

All work and no play

I was called to the Bar on August 16, 1966. Even though, as a qualified barrister, I continued to seek temporary clerical employments. A very helpful agent at one of the employment agencies near the Temple found me my first job. She was wearing a beautiful brooch of a dove, on which I commented. I worked as a dispatch clerk in an architect firm near the Holborn Station. Even as a clerk, I learned a lot about the public's feelings, specifically how they felt about British life in general in the sixties. I overheard the staff talking about the political and intelligence scandal in the early 1960s. I'm referring to the Profumo Affair, involving sex, a Russian spy, and the Secretary of State for War. The scandal captured the attention of the British public and discredited the government. It helped to topple the Conservative Party government of Prime Minister Harold Macmillan, and the Labour Party came to power in the autumn of 1964, with Harold Wilson as Prime Minister. I also overheard the staff in the architectural office talking about migrating to Australia or South Africa. I know that, eventually, many of them did. When my wife and I sailed from Cape Town to Budapest a couple of years ago, I met and talked to a few cruise passengers on board who had immigrated to South Africa in the sixties.

I also had many temporary clerical jobs at the Ministry of Social Security. The year before I started to work at the Ministry, the Supplementary Benefits Commission (part of the National Assistant Board) was merged with the Ministry of Pensions and National Insurance to form the new Ministry of Social Security. On one occasion, the Employment Agency sent me to a branch office at Battersea across the Thames. I was under the supervision of a lovely lady in this branch office. She had a boyfriend, a police officer. He would drop by very often to check on her. The manager of the branch was a trained solicitor. Just before Christmas 1966, I asked to see him. He had a spacious office that was decorated for the season. Many Christmas cards were hanging on one of the walls. I greeted him with the traditional greeting: "Merry Christmas, Sir." He knew, presumably from the employment agency, that I was a trained Barrister-at-law and was surprised that I was there working as a clerk in his branch office. I explained to him my situation. I presumed he understood and could empathize with me. In early 1967 I dropped by to tell him that I was leaving. I was going back to Sabah, where I was to complete my pupillage and simultaneously perform the function of a Deputy Public Prosecutor (DPP) in the Attorney-General Chambers. I was not yet twenty-five years old, but I looked and felt much older than my age. Stress does age us...

Junior Advocate

In Malaysia, the legal practice is fused and not separated as in England and Wales. The professionals are addressed as Advocates and Solicitors. I was in court one day. "Would you like to work in my office?" a practising Advocate and solicitor named Shelly Yap asked me. He offered me a starting salary of $1300. I did not immediately accept his offer, even though I was pleasantly surprised. I snorted! I took out a handkerchief from my trouser left pocket and blew my nose lightly to pretend I was not overly interested. Eventually, I left the Division I officer position, where I was drawing a salary of $800, and joined the firm Shelley Yap and Co. I was given a desk in the general office. I did not have a room to myself. One day my father visited me in the office and saw me among the clerical staff. Although he did not say anything, I could tell he was highly disappointed.

All practising Advocates and Solicitors had to volunteer for Legal Aids. One day as a young advocate with Shelly Yap and Co. I was assigned to defend a chap who had killed another man with a spear. He was charged with murder in the first degree. The victim was stealing his chickens. He heard some commotion below his house which was on stilts. His house was a typical Kampong house. In which one could see what was happening below through the slits on the floor above. He was enraged by the thief. Through the opening of the floor, he speared the thief from above. Unfortunately, he did not just injure the thief, which was his intention. The thief died. I believed him that there was no malice aforethought on his part. He had not planned to kill. Under the mitigating circumstances, I pleaded for him. The charge of first-degree murder was reduced to one for manslaughter.

First Committee members Sabah Law Association

I was with Shelly Yap & Co for one year. Another law firm Donaldson and Burkinshaw, was winding down their practice in Sabah. My father advanced me MYR 8000. I had enough capital to buy all the books from Donaldson and Burkinshaw and some leftover to set up my own practice on the third floor at No. 3 Neil Malcolm St. (as it was known then) in Kampong Air. This place would also serve as my residence for the next two years. While in practice, I realized that there was no governing body for the legal profession in Sabah. I immediately initiated the formation of the Sabah Law Association, drafted its Constitution, and was the First Secretary of the Association with Loo Wing Kon, the most senior advocate, as the President.

Events of 1969

Sectarian violence took place in Kuala Lumpur on that dreadful day of May 13, 1969, in the aftermath of the the1969 Malaysian General Election. The racial riot led to a declaration of a state of national emergency. The government assumed emergency powers and suspended Parliament for two years. The Malaysia Parliament would only reconvene in early 1971.

Members and friends at Sabah Friendship League

Between 1969 and 1971, a National Operations Council (NOC), also known as the Majlis Gerakan Negara (MAGERAN), was set up as a caretaker government to govern the country temporarily. Under Article 150 of the Federal Constitution, the Emergency declaration would mean that the federal government could expand its authority to any matter, including those within state governments' jurisdiction. Any Emergency Ordinance made during the proclamation also has the same effect as an Act of Parliament. One of the most well-known

Emergency Ordinance was the Emergency (Public Order and Crime Prevention) Ordinance, 1969, enacted following this May 13 riots with a provision that allowed for indefinite detention without trial. Three of my acquaintances who were members of the Sabah Friendship League (an association formed by Returning Oversea Students) were detained and imprisoned without trial in Kepayan prison under the Direction of the Director of Operation in Sabah. Tun Datu Haji Mustapha was appointed Director of Operation.

Oversea travels were also suspended, and permission to leave the country needed to be approved by the Special Advisor to the Director of Operation. One day a client of mine (originally from Sabah) called me from Hong Kong. He needed me to be in Hong Kong to negotiate and conclude a contract for him to purchase a property along Nathan Road. I had to find a way out of this predicament. I made an appointment to see the State Secretary, Mr. Richard Lind. I went to his office, and he took me to meet the Special Advisor to the Director of Operation for an interview. After the interview, I was granted permission to leave for Hong Kong. During this period, some wealthy Chinese from Sabah were also investing overseas because of Malaysia's unstable political situation. The Malay language (Bahasa Malayu) was being introduced as the official language and the compulsory medium of instruction in schools. Many thought there was no future for their children and were planning to immigrate to Canada or Australia, the two most popular countries of their choice. That, I believed, was what my father had in his mind, although he never said so>

Car enthusiast

With my car NSU Ro80 in 1972

Sabah's economic activities gradually returned after the National Operations Council's dissolution (NOC) and resumption of Parliamentary democracy. The housing sector began to bloom. A large part of my practice was in conveyancing. This involved transferring real estate legal titles from one person to another or granting encumbrances such as mortgages to commercial banks or other financing institutions. It was (still is) a legal requirement in Sabah that contracts for land sale be in writing. A typical conveyancing transaction has two major phases: the exchange of contracts and completion. The legal practice in this area was very lucrative.

As a car enthusiast, I was attracted by the elegance of the NSU Ro80. The NSU Ro80 voted Car of the Year for 1968 was a four-door sedan manufactured and marketed by the West German firm NSU from 1967 until 1977. It was noted for its innovative, aerodynamic styling by

Claus Luthe and a technologically advanced powertrain. It featured a 995-cc twin-rotor Wankel Engine driving the front wheels through a semi-automatic transmission with an innovative vacuum-operated clutch system. I bought the car, a white one, from Hong Kong when I was there negotiating a Sabah client contract. I had it shipped to KK. That was the first car I imported from overseas.

With my car Lotus Elan+ 2 S130

In 1972 I went on leave to England, my first visit since returning to Sabah after being called to the Bar in England and Wales. I visited my alma mater, The Honourable Society of the Inner Temple. While in London, I purchased the Lotus Elan +2 S130, hand-molded in glass fibre reinforced plastic. I took the car for a spin around Western Europe, covering five countries in seven days. In the year 1974, I imported a pre-owned Jensen Interceptor III. In 1979 I went to England and bought a Jaguar XJS. It was in the middle of winter. I had a close call with it because of black ice when I was driving it back to Marble Arch after an outing to Bath the day before. "These were my follies," I jokingly said, pointing at the cars to the Sabah Bank board members when they came to my house for a visit.

Jaguar XJS and Jensen Interceptor III

76 Signal Hill

My dream was to build my own house. I had already purchased a housing lot on Signal Hill from a client named Amoi binte Chinyee. She had successfully bid for this piece of land at the Government Auction a few years back. Signal Hill was zoned for low-density housing, and conditions were attached to the land title that construction of an approved dwelling must be completed within a specific time. Amoi decided not to build, so she sold the land to me.

My original house on 76 Signal Hill, KK.

In the meantime, the third floor No.3 Neil Malcolm street had served both as my law office and my residence (with Toula) for two years. Toula was a law student I met at Inner Temple. By now, she was pregnant with our daughter Selena, so we decided to rent the corner terrace house at Likas Park from my tailor Chu Chu Tailors. Toula and I have been legally separated by mutual agreement for many years. I have known May since 1969, with whom we have Nigel, hers, and ours only child. Toula has also known May as my Secretary since

1969, and both are private and decent persons. We are all friends on good terms with each other.

Out of respect for their privacy, I will not be going into details about our personal lives. Just know that May has been by my side for a long time, and I would not have it any other way. Yes, readers may feel that it has to do with trust issues or overly aloof. But there are some excellent reasons why some people choose to be private and low-key. They prefer their quiet world and have no wish to have irrelevant people and strangers in it. There is nothing wrong with that. To respect their privacy, I will not mention any more about them. While living at Likas Park, I had a cute canine, a beautiful Japanese Spitz I named Rex. One day my Rex sneaked out of the boundary fence and was run over and killed by a passing car on Tuaran Road. I lamented his untimely death. I found a suitable place on Signal Hill where my house was still under construction, and I dug a hole on the side of the hill, which was the spot where I had him royally interred.

I had already engaged Francis Wong, a friend of mine, to design a house for its construction on Signal Hill. It was estimated to cost me MYR150,000.00 to build as planned. Hoping to reduce the building cost, I asked Francis to omit the family living room on the second floor, but he was dead against it. "It will kill the whole design of this split-level house," he said. I was convinced. I accepted his advice that there be no alteration to the plans. I never regretted this decision because in the end, we spent a considerable amount of time in this family room watching television broadcasts and programs, and videos which then became available to us in the early 70s.

76 Signal Hill KK was completed in February 1972. The house was a beautifully designed 3-story building nestled on Signal Hill's slope overlooking the Sabah Sports Complex and beyond. It had wrapped-round terraces for plants and flowerpots. I had two gardeners who

worked for me part-time. They would come tender to my garden after their full-time job at the KK Town Board. One of them had green fingers. "Datuk, lihat ini (look here)". Ahmad wanted to show me the single bougainvillea plant he had grafted that bears seven different flowers.

A recent view of my house on Signal Hill.

I had lived in this house for more than twenty-five years. A few years ago, I went back to revisit Signal Hill. I saw my former house from the top of the driveway and was immensely disappointed. The House looked vastly different, with all the terraces gone, and there were no more flowers blooming on the hillside...but my memory of the place lives on....

Golfing in Kota Kinabalu

On the Links

Open Championship Cup

The year 1969 was the year I first took up the game of golf. I was already 27 years old. I bought a set of Slazenger clubs, recommended to me by David Taylor, an acquaintance of mine who was the North Borneo Trading manager in Kota Kinabalu. That was also the year I joined the Kinabalu Golf Club (KGC). Before joining KGC, I had already been practising the game, hitting golf balls at Tanjung Aru Turf Club's open field, which also served as a driving range. The driving range was run by an enterprising businessman who also owned a bookstore in Gaya street, KK. I quickly discovered I had a flair for this game. Within six months of being a member of KGC, I managed to achieve an official 18 handicap. Eventually, I would drop down to Handicap 2. I would have been what you call a scratch golfer except that The Malaysian Golf Association did not allow scratch-handicap for amateur golfers. I maintained handicap 2 for four consecutive years in the late 70s and early 80s despite my busy schedules. I had won 5 Opens which included the Opens events in Sabah, the Brunei Open, and the Sarawak Open. Some members at Sabah Golf and Country Club jokingly called me the "Pan-Borneo Champion" for a while.

I always wore white golfing pants because it is easier to match with any color golf shirt. After all, it is much cooler under the tropical sun. And people noticed that. On one occasion, I had a pair of golfing pants tailored by Chu Chu Tailors with the right side in white and the left in black- an imitation of Gary Player's idea. I was wearing this pair of pants during one of the KGC Opens at the Kinabalu Golf Club. As we approached the watering station at the 9th-hole, Police Datuk Natt's Commissioner commended on the design. "Not enough white material," I jokingly said. Tun Mustapha (then Chief Minister), who was playing in the same 4-some with Natt, standing nearby, chuckled at my joke.

Credit was due to Tun Mustapha, who in the early 1970s started the construction of the golf course at Bukit Padang, which would become Sabah Golf and Country Club (SGCC). I offered him Life Membership when I was President (1986-1989). He accepted graciously despite my refusal to support him being sworn in as the Chief Minister after the Sabah Election of 1985. The construction of the golf course stalled in 1975 when the Sabah State Elections were underway. After Berjaya won the election in 1976, and on the instruction of Datuk Harris (the new Chief Minister), some of us gathered in the conference room at KGC to decide how to continue with the golf course's construction Bukit Padang and to give it a name. I asked whether we would have just a golf course or would it also include other facilities like a tennis court etc. I suggested the name "Sabah Golf and Country Club" if we are going to have additional facilities... and the rest, as they say, is history...

Vijay Singh, the winner of the Masters 2000, the PGA Championships of 1998 and 2004, spent two months practising golf at SGCC in 1986 before taking a job at the Keningau Club in Sabah. Jim, a friend of his, asked my permission as the President of the Club for Singh to practise there. Singh had recently been suspended and banned from playing on the Asian PGA Tour in 1985 at the young age of 22. It was a period of hardship for Vijay. I believed that he ought to be given a mulligan, especially at this young age. When asked for a single word to live one's life, Confucius gives the reply: "leniency (□, *shu*)." Besides giving Vijay the permission and the opportunity to practise his game, I regularly joined him and Jim for a round of 9 holes in the late afternoons. Many years later, while in Vancouver, I read in the news that he was coming to play the 2011 RBC Canadian Open at Shaughnessy Golf & Country Club. I faxed an invitation to him requesting his company for dinner at my house. I did not get a response. I thought he might not have received the invitation, or he would be too busy as he was by now a famous golfer. After the tournament was over, I checked the Leader Board and the Final Results. His name was not on the Board. It appeared he did not turn up for this Open. The last time I saw him was at the Memorial Tournament 1998 held at Muirfield Village Golf Club in Dublin, a suburb north of Columbus, Ohio.

Jack Nicklaus was in town in 1995. He was staying at the Shangri-La Tanjong Aru Hotel in KK. He came to inspect the golf course which he had designed for a consortium of businesspeople in Sabah. The dramatic golf course was built over 200 acres (now known as The Borneo Golf Resort) in Bongawan Sabah. There was a natural lagoon that Nicklaus had cleverly integrated into his design. My friend Paul and I went to the hotel to meet him and to go with him to the golf course. I offered him the passenger bucket seat in the front of Paul's Toyota Land Cruiser and told him it was more comfortable than sitting at the back. He replied, "I don't mind where I sit," but he was happy that the front seat was offered to him, and he took it in good spirit. I was sitting directly behind him; Paul's 7-year-old son, Jeremy, was in the middle and Jack's golf designer on Jeremy's right. Unlike Arnie and Tiger Woods, some people said Jack Nicklaus is not a golf fans' golfer. I beg to differ. The car-ride to Bongawan took about an hour, and we were engaged in exciting conversations about golf courses around the world. We talked about the Turnberry Isle Resort and Club in Florida, where I told Jack I saw tangerines tree bearing fruits at the tees boxes as I went to see Senior Master in 1980. "What kind of trees are we going to have for this golf course, jack?'. In my mind, I was thinking of calamansi. "Coconut palms," Nicklaus replied. I left it at that. Jack knew golf courses. He was already involved with golf course design incredibly early on, helping Pete Dye build Harbour Town Golf Links when he was still in his late 20s. His company Nicklaus Design has designed over 410 courses in 45 countries. There were dozens of people waiting to see the famous Jack Nicklaus at the golf course he was going to inspect. Upon arrival at the Club, I tried to open the car door, but it was locked, and I muttered, "Oh, child-locked." Jack must have heard me. He got down and opened the door for me from the outside. I wondered what those fans of his who saw it were thinking? I have become an even more devoted fan of the Golden Bear ever since.

On the slopes

Skiing at San Moritz 1984

The year 1979 was the year I picked up downhill skiing. I was already 37 years old. The Chief Minister and Sabah Cabinet had granted me Sabbatical for six months. I visited my father and siblings in Canada, where they had immigrated to several years prior. I took two of my younger brothers up to Mount Seymour, a ski resort located about 40 minutes from Vancouver. Although Mount Seymour had only a small ski area, it made for the perfect day trip for us beginners. I learned to balance myself very quickly, with the similar balancing skill of water-skiing which I had acquired while a member of the Yacht Club in KK. I had shared an outboard boat with two friends of mine to learn water skiing as a recreational surface water sport in the early 70s. One day I lost my balance while skiing on one ski, and I dropped into a pool of pink jellyfish. They were Saucer-shaped. I had my life jacket on me. I stretched my hands and feet towards the sky floating on my back, and my friends circled the boat around and picked me up: Those jellyfish only gave me some itch. That is another story. Back to Mount Seymour and downhill skiing...The second time I went up Mount Seymour was with two schoolmates originally from Sung Siew School. By this second time, I was already able to ski downhill without losing balance and falling. I was even able to do Moguls. With several attempts down the Seymour slopes, I learned to maintain rhythm. I also discovered that planting my ski poles was critical when maneuvering the Moguls as the poles helped keep my rhythm and stabilized my body. I saw my two friends struggling, and they kept falling after trying to get on with their skis.

I flew with my dad to Cranbrook, British Columbia, where my brother-in-law and older sister and family lived. They were conveniently located not too far from the Fairmont Hot Springs Ski Area. My dad and my sister waited and watched my niece and I skied. There were hot springs at the base of the ski hill. This occasion was the first time I had the great pairing of activities. After the fresh powder snow skiing fun activity, immersing ourselves in a hot and steamy pool was terrific. We finished off our day with one of the best skis and soak in North America - with a revitalizing soak in the mineral hot pools.

At the "Snow Bowl" Obertauern

In the early '80s, I ventured farther into European ski resorts. I have done ski-in and ski-out at Saa Fee, a ski resort set up high on the Swiss Alps. It was comparatively a small ski resort, but the views were fabulous everywhere, and the village was just lovely. On another occasion staying in a small hotel in Obertauern Ski resort near Salzburg, I asked for the bill after drinking at the bar. "You pay when you check out the bartender said. He pinned the bill on a corkboard behind him, where I saw many bills pinned on that board. That was in 1983. People were so trusting. Obertauern was Austria's snowiest village with snow depth more than many other resorts, even more than the world-famous San Moritz, where I spent a couple of days skiing with my daughter after I had attended a conference in Zurich. But whereas when we were in Obertauern, I would wake up early in the morning, looked out of the window from the tiny room where we stayed for two weeks, and would see the thick powdery layer of snow covering everything in sight. It was nicknamed "Snow Bowl."

I kept the same Ellesse Ski jacket and pants for more than 20 years. I never had the desire nor felt the need to buy a new ski suit, even though I had seen many fashionable skiers wearing the much-advertised Helly Hansen collections. The colour and design of mine were a bit dated by the turn of the 21st century. I had attracted some curious skiers and onlookers at ski resorts in more recent times. Age is catching on. I no longer ski at Whistler, even though it is less than two hrs-drive from we live. The last time I went out skiing was at Big White Ski Resort near Kelowna in 2002 with some Singapore relatives. It seems so long ago. The snow condition at Big White usually is better than in Whistler. It is powdery, but it was cold when we were there. At the top, where we got off from the lift chair, it was minus 25 degrees Celsius

With my horse Trident at the stable in Tanjung Aru KK.

Back to Horse Riding

In early 1974 May told me the husband of a friend of hers in Kuala Lumpur had a horse that he would give me if I had it ship over to KK. He would like to give me this horse if I could pay for it to be shipped over to KK. It was an Australian thoroughbred, a racing horse by the name of "Olympic Triumph." Well, the horse apparently had not lived up to his name - hence the owner, Mr. Looi, was prepared to part company with him. I accepted Looi's offer, and he shipped it over to me. The horse was quarantined somewhere in Inanam for the required period before taking him over to the Tanjung Aru Turf Club. I renamed him "Trident." Before Trident, I had already been riding a Bajau pony from Kota Belud. I retired the pony. I put Trident in the same stable and taught the stable hand who used to attend to the pony how to feed and look after Trident.

With a Bajau pony on Tanjung Aru Beach

On Trident's first outing, I walked, trotted, and then slowly cantered him around the Tanjung Aru Turf Club's racetrack. As soon as we made the turn, he galloped full speed home. He would do this every time I took him out on the track. I had a challenging time pulling at the rein to rein him in. He was a racehorse, and that was instinct, and he had been trained over the years to do that. I learned from Captain Somosky and his horses that different horses act differently. Unfortunately, Trident was a stubborn one. "Whoa Whoa" and "Stop it, Trident," I yelled at him. I pulled on his bit as we made the bend on the racetrack home. I gave him carrots and spoke softly to him, but it did not work. It took me a couple of months, with carrots and stick, so to speak, to break his habits. Eventually, he learned, and I always patted him on his neck before and after the ride. Finally, I turned him into a wonderful riding horse. He seemed to understand my riding choices, and we became a team.

With Trident on Tanjung Aru Beach

People in the coffee shops at Tanjung Aru town would see me walk and trot him on the side of the road and across the football field to the Tanjung Aru beach. Another group of spectators from the KGC and the Yacht Club would take over with wide protuberant eyes. One day I met the Hong Kong & Shanghai Bank Manager's wife outside her residence by the beach. I stopped Trident and chatted with her. She looked at Trident and asked: "Do you know what he is thinking?". I said I wished I knew. But Trident was able to understand me when I talked to him. The Tanjung Aru Beach was uncrowded in those days. That was in the early 70s, and the Shangri-La Hotel had not yet been built. I was able to trot and canter him on the beach. Trident loved the beach and loved the softness of the sand under his hoofs. He was indeed an excellent companion for several years. But eventually, I was getting busy as the Attorney-General, and I had to travel often to Kuala Lumpur or out of state. On one sad day, I spoke with my stable hand about retiring Trident. He retired Trident to someone's pasture in Kota Belud.

With a Cayuse horse at Pemberton, B. C.

Years later, I got on the back of a cayuse horse in Pemberton, British Columbia, with Copper Cayuse Outfitters, a horseback riding tour company. It had been almost 40 years since my last ride with Trident. Even though I was an experienced rider, I was not sure of myself after such a long time not having been on the back of a horse. I was even more anxious about handling this cayuse. If I remember, his name was "Reno." I was not sure how Reno would react. But he quickly sensed my ability and confidence and seemed to know my riding need. We got on very well. With me was May, on horseback for the first time in her life. So, Kathy, who walked the other horse with May on its back for a while around the ground, decided we would do some easy trials. We tracked through the forest, into and over a creek, and even saw some deer in the distance. When we got to the open field, I had the chance and was able to do a bit of cantering. It was different from riding on the beach, but it reminded me of the time I spent with Captain Somosky in Wimbledon and Richmond Park.

Election Nominations

Sabah was and still is governed under the Parliamentary System. Sabah People's United Front (Parti Bersatu Rakyat Jelata Sabah), commonly known by its abbreviation BERJAYA was a political party based in Sabah's State. Since its start on July 15th, 1975, Berjaya had been a Barisan Nasional (BN) partner, then federal ruling coalition in Malaysia. Datuk Harris Salleh formed Berjaya, joined by Tun Fuad Stephens, a former Malaysian High Commissioner to Australia. During the Sabah State Election of 1976, as the legal advisor to the Berjaya, I was flown all over the West Coast to check the Party's candidates' nomination papers. Political parties had learned a lesson. In the 1971 State Elections, all nominated candidates of opposition parties were disqualified on technical grounds – errors found in their nomination papers. Berjaya was aware of this and therefore emphasized that the nomination papers for their candidates were correctly filled out and executed to prevent kerfuffle in nomination centres on nomination day.

The Party charted a twin-engine Cessna plane from the Flying Club. We could not return to base on one of those trips because the Kota Kinabalu airport was closed during an emergency. We were informed that the Moro National Liberation Front (an armed insurgent group committed to setting up an independent Mindanao) from the Philippines was seeking land in KK airport. Three of us (the pilot, my female assistant, and I) were stranded and had to share a small room in a little hotel in Kota Belud for the night. The pilot did not sleep well because he was worried about the plane being left unattended and parked overnight. He got up at the first break of daylight to check on it and reported back to us that everything was fine. Tensions were high, and a lot at stake for Sabahans. On the night before the nomination, Berjaya sent two "security guards" to my house to ensure safety.

I was holding the nomination paper of Tun Fuad Stephens with whom I would accompany, in the following morning, to the nomination Centre in Tuaran.

Election Nomination Centre Tuaran

Appointment of Attorney-General

A few of us gathered in the study in the house of Datuk Harris at Likas Bay. We were waiting for the results of the 1976 Sabah State Elections. Results were trickling in, being related to us by phones by poll watchers at the polling centres. There was absolute euphoria when we realized that Berjaya had won – First Past the Post. Tun Fuad did something I would never forget. Firstly, he called his children studying in Australia, "You are speaking with the Chief Minister..." he said over the phone. After his conversation with his children, he turned to me and said: "I want you to be the Attorney-General." I looked at him but did not give him a reply. He said, "think about it." I had to because I had a lucrative law practice. I needed to arrange for someone to run the law firm. At the Istana's swearing ceremony for the Chief Minister and his Cabinet Ministers, I gave him the response. "Yes, I accept your offer to be A-G."

I did not ask for it, but someone in the Secretariat had already arranged my Contract of Service and remunerations with inducement benefits. This appointment was not without political repercussion in Sabah. Constitutionally, the State Attorney-General's position needed the federal Government's approval, which was given without unnecessary delay. My appointment was the first "political" appointment to the Attorney-General's post, which had hitherto always been held by a senior officer of the Judicial or Legal Service. This appointment became a precedent that successive governments have since followed. I served as the Attorney-General for five years. After Berjaya won for a second term in 1981, my contract was renewed with revised terms for remunerations and benefits for another five.

Tragedy

On the morning of June 5th, 1976, I was not feeling well. I had this terrible cold. It had been bothering me for days. It started with my allergy, which I was prone to, whether it was dust or pollens. Tun Fuad Stephens, as the Chief Minister, was going off to Labuan. He was going to meet the federal Minister Finance, who was also the Chairman of Petronas (Malaysian Government wholly owned oil and gas company). My driver drove me to the airport to see him off. With me in the VIP lounge at the airport was also his brother Ben Stephens, the protocol officer, and few departmental heads. I was sitting next to him on the sofa. When I realized I was close to him and because of my flu, I moved away instinctively to a single chair. Tun told me to go home for a rest. After seeing him off, I took his advice and went straight home to recover from my ailment.

By the afternoon, the day after, I felt much better, so I went to the Kinabalu Golf Club to meet up with some members for a snooker game. I was still not up to par for golf. I could not concentrate on the snooker game either and lost my wagers. It was a stressful time, and I felt a strong urge to be left alone for a while and to clear my thoughts. Too many things had happened. I found out also that those hard days often drove me back to Nature. Not just the little sights and sounds are seen and heard while sitting alone under the small coconut palms of KGC. Not even by looking out at Gaya Island or into the South

Sea with the help of a jug of Anchor beer. I drove to an area off-road and parked in the shade under the ponderosa trees by the beach. This spot was where I was familiar with and to which I had been many times before. It was late in the afternoon, and the sun was still above the horizon. As I reflected, I heard a stalled plane's splattering sound, and then I heard no more. It was quiet again by the beach. I sat for a while, reflecting and enjoying this location's quietness, and then drove home.

Early evening, I received a phone call from someone: "Datuk Harris wants to talk to you. Can you please come to the Secretariat?" I cannot recall who telephoned me. I just cannot remember. It was most likely the Cabinet Secretary at that time. I sensed that something significant must have happened. It must be for a meeting, but I was not informed of the purpose. Upon my arrival, I saw Datuk Harris, Hamid Egoh (State Secretary), Datuk Abdul Rahman bin Ya'kub (Chief Minister of Sarawak), and a couple of Sabah Cabinet Ministers. The Commissioner of police Yusof Khan told me that Chief Minister Tun Fuad Stephens and several Cabinet Ministers had been killed in an air crash a short while ago. He Yusof Khan (with some police officers) was on the spot immediately after it happened. The news was a complete shock to me. I learned that a close friend of mine, Wahid Peter Andu, the Permanent Secretary of Finance, also perished in the accident. I tried to compose myself. When he observed that I had regained my composure, he prompted me to advise Datuk Harris to be sworn in as soon as possible as the new Chief Minister. We both knew that we needed a Head of Government for direction.

The Oath of Office and the Instrument of Appointment of Chief Minister were in Bahasa Malaysia, a language I had poor knowledge of. I looked at the documents and The Chief Minister of Sarawak, himself a barrister from Lincoln's Inn, sensing that I had a problem with the language, graciously helped me go through the text. We then left for the Istana, and Harris bin Mohd Salleh was sworn in as the 6th Chief Minister of Sabah.

The conspiracy theory

An incident that has generated many conspiracy theories over the years is the tragedy of June 6, 1976, because a plane carrying the Chief Minister and a few Cabinet Ministers had crashed. Different government teams carried out series of investigations. As the Attorney-General, I was given a copy of the confidential report on the incident's investigation. The Australian GAF Nomad manufacturer also launched their analysis to prove that the crash was not due to a mechanical defect. My recollection was that the investigating teams did not reveal any technical errors or sabotage as being the cause of the air crash. At that time, what was discovered by them was that the accident was due to human error and that the plane lost control when it tried to land because it was carrying goods above the maximum load. These, though not sensational, were the findings. Many news outlets played it as a big story as they should because a Chief Minister and some cabinet members died in this tragedy. Some other readers may take this as just a story. But it is a story not without political impact for many years. I am aware that at any given point in time, some will continue to poke their fingers at the authorities for not releasing the findings of this crash or drive into the eyes of news media that the most important story never really got covered.

Unlike some ancient and epic stories we have read or been told, this story of the Double Six Tragedy may soon be forgotten in the sand of time. Old stories have survived all these years because those stories were in an uncluttered literary world. We have now crossed over some invisible boundary. We no longer read. We are floundering in the internet world for "knowledge." Today is the age of misinformation overload, and we now live without clarity over which information or news is credible and which is not. It is hard to separate the wheat from the chaff, the good from the bad, the trivial from the important. Indeed, we are not even sure what news is blocked and kept away from us by big Techs!

Yayasan Sabah Tower

The Tun Mustapha Tower.

In 1979, during my sabbatical, the Secretariat was moved to the Yayasan Building (renamed Tun Mustapha Tower) located by Likas Bay, about 5 km away from the Kota Kinabalu City Centre. The Tower is a 122-metre circular tower of steel and glass tall building, constructed in 1977 by Mori Building Company, a Japanese builder. It has a central core with steel brackets supporting each floor. The building was named Yayasan Sabah Tower as it housed Yayasan Sabah, a state-sponsored Foundation established to promote education and economic development in the state. When completed in 1977, it was one of only three such buildings in the world based on this design concept. The whole complex housed an auditorium, two mini-theatres, an exhibition foyer, a gymnasium, and a kindergarten. The

Attorney-General's offices, together with a law library, were located on the 9th floor.

I had a Mercedes Benz assigned to me as an official car with a driver, but I always preferred to drive my private vehicle, especially the Jaguar XJS I had just imported from England. It was an exciting and interesting time. One day, I left my Jaguar XJS parked at the Plaza of Yayasan Sabah and entered the Yayasan Building's podium to lift to my office. One of the security guards chased after me to let me know that parking was not allowed on the plaza. Walking to the life t at the same time with me was one of my legal assistants Richard Malanjum who would eventually become the ninth Chief Justice of Malaysia. I told the guard it would be just for a short while because I was in a rush. Richard looked at the guard and saw his reaction. The guard did not know I was the Attorney-General, but he was just doing his job.

Onboard LACIII (Puteri Berjaya)

On this occasion, I had to rush because soon I would be flying off to Miami to conclude the deal to purchase a Yacht for the Istana and take delivery. It was a long 26-hour flight from Kota Kinabalu via London to Miami. Despite still being groggy from Jetlag, I neverthe-less went straight to the office of Mr. Carver, the yacht owner. He had a memento on his desk that reads: "Remember the golden rule; the man who has the gold makes the rule." I wondered whether he saw my frown as I glanced at it while trying to control myself from smiling. He looked pleasant, not unlike a politician. He did not change his mask from a cheerful smile to deal with our serious conversation. I thought that he was an absolute expert in facial calibration. I couldn't know what he was thinking just by looking at the expression on his face. Carver had his female pilot flew me to Belize in his private jet. We flew there to officially take delivery of the yacht bought by the Sabah Government for the Instana. Captain Brian Coen, his wife Angela, and several deckhands were waiting for me. Eventually, Brian would skipper the yacht all the way to Kota Kinabalu, escorted by the marines through the treacherous Philippines water, which was known to be infested with pirates. We renamed the Yacht from LAC III to Puteri Berjaya.

Around that time, I had an American law student assigned to my office the Yayasan Building by the Asia Foundation. His name was Kevin Dwyer. Kevin had an uncle, a Catholic priest from Washington, who came to Sabah for a visit. When he called at my office at the Yayasan Building, we talked about President Marcos. We both realized it was not easy to govern a country of 8000 islands. Kevin had many stories. He was detained at the Narita Airport on the way from the United States. It was a case of misidentification because of the name. Kevin's friends from college visited him, and I brought them to climb Mount Kinabalu, the tallest mountain in South East Asia, measuring 14,355 feet. I could not make it to the top of the mountain because I was suffering from altitude sickness at about 11,000 feet, where we were staying for the night. One of Kevin's friends, a medical student, recommended that I not proceed with the group to the summit the following morning. I took his advice and waited for them before we descended together. Eventually, Kevin went back to Washington DC and worked in a law firm that required him to travel to Africa. A few years later, I received the sad news that he died of Gangrene.

The Silent Riot

With traditional Kadazan Headgear

As the Attorney-General, you could say I was well known, but still, I figured many people could not recognize me if I walked in town. I used to walk along Gaya Street. Sometimes I would turn around and walk back to the car. Still, sometimes I would enter the shop and sit for a while. Not so much for the coffee, but mainly to feel like a fly on the wall. To listen to conversations going on around me, hearing, for instance, a conversation between a couple who spoke intermittently in their native tongue and sometimes in English. "Tidak boleh manang lah (cannot win lah)". That way, I somehow was able to gauge what was going on in people's minds in Sabah.

Party Berjaya, the party, formed in 1975 to oust Tun Mustapha from office, was now in the second term. The Party had an impressive victory in the 1981 Election, winning 44 out of 48 seats. Everything seemed to be flying high for the Party's politicians, including its

President Datuk Harris, who had made Labuan a Federal Territory. Perhaps the transfer of Labuan to Federal Territory should have been by consultation, with debates in the Legislative Assembly and maybe even a referendum. But things appeared to be fine on the surface for Berjaya. However, there was deep discontent among the native Kadazans with the abrogation of the Tambunan district status. I remember warning the Chief Minister about this move.

Sabah Native Cultural dance

The Kadazans form the largest ethnic group in Sabah. Joseph Pairin, the Hougan Siou (paramount leader of the Kadazans), was an original Berjaya member. Because of policy differences, he broke away from the party and formed Parti Bersatu Sabah (PBS). When the State election was called in 1985, Berjaya was toppled by newcomers PBS. It was an unprecedented event in Malaysian politics. Not only because of the unexpected defeat of Berjaya by PBS, a party formed barely 47 days before the State elections but also what was to follow the election. On the night of the 1985 state election power struggle took place at the Istana. Some viewed it as a "coup." This "coup" would be seldom talked about today. However, this was the precursor to the destructive demonstrations the following year, the 48 days of civil unrest in Sabah - termed as the "Silent Riot."

What happened on the night of the Election in 1985? Much of what transpired on the night of the Sabah State Election (1985) have been revealed in a court case. The case Tun Datu Haji Mustapha bin Datu Harun vs. Yang Di-Pertua Negeri Sabah Mohamed Adnan Robert & Datuk Joseph Pairin Kitingan (No2), (1986) 2 MLJ 420, OCJ Kota Kinabalu. I testified as a witness to what happened. I was examined, crossed examined, and reexamined for many days in court by abled Queen Counsels from England. In fact, the questionings took so long that they were wearing down on me physically. His Lordship, the presiding judge, must have noticed. He said to me, "You may sit if you prefer." Allowing me to sit in the witness stand instead of standing all the time during questioning. Counsels on both sides noticed this gesture. Later, during the short recess, one of the counsels commented that it was rather unusual. Be that as it may, I was grateful for the empathy on the judge's part for this witness.

Sabah Bank Berhad

By 1986 I was again back to law practice in the law firm I started almost twenty years ago. One day in early 1987, I received a call from a Senior Advisor to Bank Negara (the Central Bank of Malaysia) asking me whether I would be appointed Chairman of the Board for Sabah Bank. The Sabah Bank, incorporated in 1979 and majority Government-owned, was under financial stress caused by non-performing loans. As the Bank of Final Resort, Bank Negara had to step in to rescue the Sabah Bank and protect the depositors. A sum to the tune of one hundred and fifty million (MYR150,000,000.00) was injected into Sabah Bank to shored up its capital. Bank Negara wanted new stewardship. I was hesitant at first but was assured that I would have the support of a new Board of Directors. I had no banking background and experience, even though a significant part of our law firm's practice involved capital finance, loans, and mortgages, and general conveyancing within the banking sector. I had already managed to put us on the approved panel of legal advisors of fourteen (14) financial institutions. I was honoured by this offer for Chairmanship of Sabah Bank Berhad but at the same time felt humbled and inadequate.

Chairman's office Sabah Bank

The Chairman's office and the Board Room of Sabah Bank were housed on the top floor of one of the three towers at the junction of Karamusing. It was spacious and lavishly furnished with Italian-designed furniture. On June 17, 1987, I was invited to attend the Board Meeting of Sabah Bank. Bank Negara had already by then approved my appointment. But I was still waiting for the approval of the other directors' appointments so that whoever they were could come on board. Bank Negara had proposed a former Chief Executive of the Malayan Bank, a prominent economist, an accountant, and a lawyer to join the new Board of Sabah Bank. I informed Bank Negara that I was still waiting for the directors to be approved by the Federal Minister of Finance. A senior Advisor of Bank Negara told me that he would personally call on the Finance Minister, which he did, and shortly after that, we received the approval. From then on, I had the valuable help and expertise of my fellow Board members.

Members of Board of Directors, Sabah Bank Berhad

I was interviewed by the Union of Employees of Sabah Bank officers soon after I took office. I had already found out that the Sabah Bank, particularly at the Head office, was overstaffed. They understood when I assured them I had no intention of retrenching any staff even though, in my mind, I thought it would be good for the Bank to trim some fat, so to speak. However, I told them that I expected them to be redeployed to other branches if required. In my address to the Bank staff at the first Annual Dinner, I asked them to imagine our institution's corporate structure (as a triangle) not with the Chairman at the top. That our institution is an upside-down triangle, the important people at the top would be the front-line workers, the tellers, cashiers, and all the staff having direct contacts with the public. I issued new administration directives and loan guidelines. It was not an easy task for us to restructure and manage the Bank. It reminded me of a juggler's performance who keeps spinning plates on the tips of many wands and trying to keep them aloft. With my fellow directors' help and the staff's cooperation, we managed to turn the Bank around in three years. By 1989 Sabah Bank was no longer in the red.

Conferences, Merger and Acquisition

With Program attendees, lecturers, and staff.

In the interim, Bank Negara had the vision for smaller banks in Malaysia to merge to form larger corporations to compete globally. With that in mind, Sabah Bank was gradually restructured to merge with other financial institutions in Malaysia. To keep abreast of the financial market in Asia and the rest of the world, Bank Negara had suggested that CEOs of banks attend one regional and one overseas economic conference a year.

I attended programs for this purpose at the New York Institute of Finance, Harvard Institute of International Development (HIID), and the prestigious INSEAD at Fontainebleau France for "Mergers and Acquisitions" and "Strategic Management in Banking." I told the classes where I attended that I had no idea why Bank Negara appointed me Chairman of a bank. Unlike attendees at these Programs, mostly coming from the banking sector, I had no banking experience. "Every problem presents a business opportunity," said the professor at Harvard. Unfortunately, HIID got itself involved in a Russian scandal. The President of the institute resigned in 1999 to form the Center for International Development (CID). A task force was appointed in July 1999 to review the future of the HIID. The Institute has since been dissolved, with its functions distributed to faculties within Harvard University. What led HIID to its demise was partly due to the Russian conflict of interest scandal, structural problems, and financial deficits - Harvard Institute for International Development - Wikipedia. https://en.wikipedia.org/wiki/Harvard_Institute_for_International_Development

At Pound Hall Harvard University

I recalled one time I was asked by a lecturer at INSEAD how I would gauge a candidate for a merger or acquisition. I went in front of the class and wrote the word "CAMEL" on the board. I learned that "CAMEL" is easily remembered as the acronym for Capital, Assets, Management, Equity, and Liquidity, which I had picked up reading about Central Banks' function in their assessment of financial institutions. That I presumed would also be a good yardstick to measure a candidate's worth to be acquired. It was pretty fun saying that to my class at INSEAD, especially to my newfound acquaintances Nassir and Mohammed from Egypt. Later I told them about my experience of riding a camel at the Sphinx in Egypt years ago.

At INSEAD Fontainebleau, France

My classmates at INSEAD were mainly middle-aged men, with some in their thirties, but they were still very keen soccer players. So, they arranged among themselves to play soccer after class. It was not my cup of tea. I just sat around, watched, and cheered. I did talk to a couple of the Swiss bankers about skiing in Switzerland. A few of us would typically go out together for dinners. They would decide what wine to order, and looking at me, they would say in jest: "Nick, you choose the water." I laughed and would pick Avian without fail. In addition to immersing myself in the banking world and learning more about Finance, I had also enriched myself around personal relationships - with people from around the world. After I returned to Sabah, I wrote them the following letter:

"10 June 1993

The Class of (tired Bankers) 1993

INSEAD

Greetings to everyone!

It was indeed an enjoyable time I spent with you at INSEAD. I am honoured and delighted to have made your acquaintances, and I sincerely hope we will have the opportunity to meet again. Most of you, especially Bern-Albrecht, I am sure, will survive the INSEAD ideas of improving the banking world. The first casualty, no doubt, will be me. After INSEAD, I spent two weeks of gorgeous summer holidays in Banff and the surrounding areas near the Canadian Rockies. All of you are overworked, and I suggest you do the same.

Frank said he would be taking the family to see the (recently bombed) World Trade Centre in New York. Frank, frankly, I think you are going to the wrong place. You might want to come to Sabah (while I am still around). Joao has already indicated that he would like a golf match with meat the Sabah Golf and Country Club. (playing off his Crocodile 14 handicap). He asked me whether it was safe there. Well, the street of Kota Kinabalu Sabah is safer than the streets of my favourite city London (sorry to team-mate Colin). I would not compare it with Sao Palo (after hearing from Sebastiao that he could not walk in the street). How did you manage to meet all the pretty Brazilian girls if you were not allowed to walk?

As for Nasir and Mohammed, the greenery of Sabah will be refreshing. If it rains, you can have my umbrella (no need to return them). You do not have to bring a tent, although a camel will be welcome. You know out of the 18 participants, only Chris and not Werner (my team-mate) had been to Malaysia. Urs spent a spell in Thailand (that is not the same as we are unspoiled). Urs, I would like to join you in Turkey one day. Before I get older (I did not figure whether I was the oldest in the class), although Sebastiao said I looked it! I might take on Hans-Joerg's offer for free sky-dive with him. But Rod, how would you like to scuba-dive in the Sabah waters (look at the enclosed brochures)? Better and more interesting than your diving in the used mine in Frankfurt. The practice in Frankfurt will keep you in shape, though.

Eddy, it was fun meeting you. You tried too hard at soccer. Would you still want Colin to be a coach? I do hope you will forgive me for "shortening" the meaning of "Buyer's Market" for you. If I want a good dinner in Europe (I mean an expensive one!) I know how to call for Guido and Rinus, the wine connoisseurs. Patrick will be invited, provided he tells more of his Irish jokes. I will go to Coral Gables for dinner and look up Oscar. Janos, I have mentioned you to my brother-in-law. If he visits Hungary, I hope you can recommend him some places for him to see. I may join him on the trip as well.

All of you chaps are welcome to visit me. I may be calling it quit at banking soon, although the relevant costs will no doubt survive. I have worked for 30 years. First as a teacher, then as Advocate and Solicitor, for nine years, after reading law and being called to the English Bar (the pubs as well) in 1966. I was Attorney-General for Sabah from 1976-1985. I have been in banking since (after being roped in by Bank Negara as Chairman of the Board of Directors to rescue the then failed Sabah Bank). It is now time to go trout or salmon fishing for the rest of my life. Please do not be surprised if you find me in your neighbourhood, even in Stuttgart, where Frank is thinking of retiring.

With Best Wishes to you All

Nicholas"

By 1997 Sabah Bank was already a profitable bank generating a healthy balance sheet. It was a workable candidate for suitors or takeovers. Initially, I desired that Bank Negara would agree to divest and have the bank listed on the Stock Exchange in Kuala Lumpur. However, in the end, in the Central Bank's wisdom to which I subscribed, it was better to merge it with some other financial institutions to form a larger corporation. The merger created what is today The Alliance Bank of Malaysia.

MAJAPS (Council of the Justices of Peace Sabah)

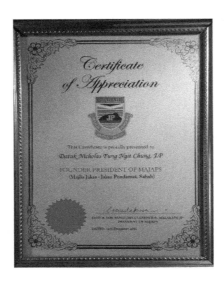

From the Chairman's chair in Sabah Bank, I could look out to the harbour, Gaya Island, and beyond. I got up from my chair, stood by the window, shifted my eyes to the nearer objects, to Karamusing warehouses, to where the bombs went off during the riots of 1986. As my eyes shifted, my mind wandered, and I reflected on the riots. The riots occurred in response to the 1985 Sabah State Election results, whereby the newly formed Parti Bersatu Sabah (PBS) won, ousting Berjaya from the helm of government. Because of political maneuverings, the Assemblymen of PBS started to defect. Chief Minister Joseph Pairin (President of PBS) called a snap election. It was held on 4th and 5th May 1986. PBS won again, and this time with a more significant margin. It was reported (uncensored) that the mobs took to the streets to try to bring down the president of PBS, Joseph Pairin, from the Chief Minister post. - 1986 Sabah riots - Wikipedia. https://en.wikipedia.org/wiki/1986_Sabah_riots

Peace came to my mind as I was looking out from my office window in Sabah Bank. At some stages in my life, I have been called a "peacenik." I had already been appointed as a Justice of the Peace in Sabah. But what is a JP? I realized that yearly, on the birthday of His Excellency the Yang di-Pertua Negara (Head of State), more Justices of the Peace were being appointed. I felt the need for an association of JPs.

Consequently, I initiated the formation of the Council of the Justices of Peace Sabah (MAJAPS). I wrote to all surviving JPs appointed by the Colonial government of North Borneo and invited them to join the Association which I had intended to form. Mr. John Baxter, who was in Keningau at that time, declined because of his advanced age but supported the idea. Datuk Peter Yew, who the colonial government also appointed, accepted and was a member of my protem committee. I am grateful to Lawrence Thien Shin Hing J.P. (now "Datuk"), who helped in the Council's formation. After I retired from the President's post, the eminent leader Clarence B. Malakun J.P. (now Tan Sri) took over the helm and continued to steer it along. "Peace" is the operative word in the Council of JPs. To my mind, being appointed a JP is not merely an honour or award. Every JP must ensure that the law of the land is upheld and peace is preserved for the common good.

Free Pilgrim

I was 55 years old, considered young by Western countries' standards for retirement. But at that time, it was the retirement age for most public servants in Malaysia and in that part of the world. I had always thought of eventually retiring to Canada. It was a country of choice that my father and many of my siblings had immigrated to many years ago. By now, with May, I had a young son Nigel who was of school-age going to preschool in Vancouver and ready to ring the church bell at St. John's the Apostle Church in Port Moody. I wanted to spend more time with the family instead of being an "astronaut" (a pejorative term for an absentee father who continues to work in his native country after his whole family has already immigrated to a new country). I wrote to Bank Negara, informing them that I wished to seek early retirement. The Board had approved, and the Central Bank also agreed that I receive suitable gratuity. So, I retired and became a *"Free Pilgrim,"* and my "journey" then truly began.

I am now smelling the roses and no longer wearing a tie or a court band. I travel light and globetrot around the world, trying to counter bigotry by sharing and enjoying stories in a constant search for an inner spiritual path. I try letting people know that peace can be achieved even though there are differences among us. My "journey" has been documented in three books: Free Pilgrim, Free Pilgrim 2, and Free Pilgrim 3, and the stories continue...This story is not an autobiography. At the beginning of this story, I mentioned that a true autobiography is one which the writer would like only the Almighty God to be the only reader. This is just another story, snapshots and snippets of a part of my lifelong journey...and this journey continues... Come and walk with me...

About The Author

Born in 1942 in British North Borneo (Sabah Malaysia) and now residing in Vancouver, British Columbia, Canada, Nicholas Fung was trained as a Barrister-at-Law at the Honourable Society of The Inner Temple. He was called to the Bar of England and Wales in 1966 and eventually returning to Sabah, where he has served as the State Attorney-General. He initiated the formation and was the first Secretary of the then Sabah law Association. He was the founder and first President of The Council of Justices of The Peace and a founding member and President of Sabah Golf and Country Club.

Appointed by Bank Negara (Central Bank of Malaysia) as Chairman and Chief Executive of Sabah Bank Berhad, he was tasked with restructuring the bank (which has since merged with Alliance Bank Malaysia), and it is from that position that he ultimately retired. He has since traveled the world as a *"Free Pilgrim."* He has published three books entitled *Free Pilgrim*, *Free Pilgrim2,* and Free Pilgrim 3, documenting his *"journey"* with insightful photographs and writings that clearly illustrate both the divine and mundane nature of humanity. He reawakens our drive to discover new places, learn about new cultures, and maybe even better understand who we are as a human collective. That we are all one people, and even though separated by continents and millennia, our humanity shines through our great works and a shared appreciation for beauty, reason, and the world around us.

CPSIA information can be obtained
at www.ICGtesting.com
Printed in the USA
BVHW020729160921
616188BV00016B/39

9 781039 113749